Strawberry wine with cherry: inheritance of wings
A silenced story

AUTHOR NOTE

The word "silenced" is misspelled on the original cover on purpose.

It represents a person quieted so long that even the word begins to lose its voice.

Take a red marker and cross it out

become part of the protest against silence.

Table of Contents

COPYRIGHT
INTRODUCTION
—Why I Wrote This Book
PROLOGUE
- Inheritance of Wings
Purpose: To tell the whole truth with grace and strength.
CHAPTER 1. PG.1-7
 - Cherry: The Stolen Glow
Her light became My map through darkness.
CHAPTER 2. PG.8-12
-The Family Pattern
The inheritance of pain disguised as loyalty.
CHAPTER 3.PG.13-19
- Before the Separation
 I learned early that love and survival weren't the same thing.
CHAPTER 4. PG.20-26
 - The Attempt at Age Twelve
A childhood mistaken for servitude and the first spark of rebellion.
CHAPTER 5. PG.27-34
 - When She Saw
The first moment My mother saw My pain clearly and chose to fight for Me.
CHAPTER 6. PG.35-39
 - The Day She Came Back for Me
 Love surviving even as the mind fades the body present, but the spirit slipping away.
CHAPTER 7. PG.40-45
- The Month of Hunger
Hunger wasn't just about food it was for freedom, safety, and love.
CHAPTER 8. PG.46-51
- The Streets Taught Me
- The streets became both my enemy and your teacher.
CHAPTER 9. PG.52-58
 - The One I Loved Most (My First Yes)

Love and loss exist in the same breath.
CHAPTER 10. PG.59-64
- The Ones Who Broke the Meaning of Love
Healing through time, trust, and faith.
CHAPTER 11. PG.65-73
 - My Brother's Shadow
When family becomes both witness and wound.
CHAPTER 12. PG.74-79
- I Won't Be Garbage
Defiance as rebirth.
CHAPTER 13. PG.80-84
 - Something to Live For
Motherhood as redemption.
CHAPTER 14. PG.85-88
- The Ghosts That Stay
Remembrance as strength.
CHAPTER 15. PG.89-93
 - Memory and Re-Creation
Turning memory into a living legacy.
CHAPTER 16. PG.94-98
 - The Streets to Salvation
Redemption through faith, not perfection.
CHAPTER 17. PG.99-104
- Strawberry Wine with Cherry
Love as the taste that never faded.
CHAPTER 18. PG.105-110
 - Inheritance of Wings (Finale)
Flying beyond the story that tried to keep me grounded.
EPILOGUE. PG.111-116
 - For the Next Generation
Legacy rebuilt on truth and love.

Reflection
A lifetime of pain has taught me this

The more they tried to break me, the more I understood why my mother couldn't heal.
Every scar they left on me was one I recognized in her and in every person who was born into pain they were too young to name.

This story isn't just about mothers and daughters.
It's about anyone who became a mirror for the wounds that raised them those who carried the weight of hands that never learned gentleness, and the silence that follows when the world pretends not to see.

It's for the children who grew up inside the same storm that once swallowed their parents whole for those who learned love and fear in the same breath.

Abuse doesn't always end when it's over.
It lingers in the voices we hear when we doubt ourselves, in the choices we make out of survival instead of peace.
It passes through generations like an echo, until someone is brave enough to stop and listen.

I am that pause.
I am the breath between what was done and what no longer has to be repeated.

This book isn't about blame it's about truth, and what it takes to face it.
It's about every soul who refused to let pain be the only thing they inherited.

To those still stuck in systems of silence I see you.
To those who survived without healing you are not broken you were conditioned.
And to those trying to unlearn what hurt taught you this story is your reflection too.

 Strawberry Wine with Cherry

by Carissa Horton

Copyright Page

Copyright © 2025 by Carissa Horton
All rights reserved.No part of this book may be reproduced or transmitted in any form or by any means electronic, mechanical, photocopying, recording, or otherwise without prior written permission from the author, except in the case of brief quotations used in reviews or critical articles.This book is a true account of real events and lived experiences.Certain names, identifying details, and locations have been changed to protect the privacy and safety of those involved.For information, contact Carissa Horton

Disclaimer

This book is based on true events. Every story, emotion, and experience written within these pages is real and lived. Only certain names and locations have been changed to protect privacy and personal safety. These pages contain accounts of trauma, abuse, and loss that may be difficult to read, but they are told with honesty and purpose to bring understanding, not harm. This book was written as a form of healing and truth telling, not accusation or revenge. If you recognize parts of yourself or your story here, know that this book was born from pain transformed into peace. It exists to break silence, not to reopen wounds.

Introduction
Why I Wrote This Book

This book is my truth the story I wasn't allowed to tell while it was happening.

For years, I watched people rewrite my mother's story, and then mine twisting our pain into something that made them comfortable. They called her unstable, dramatic, ungrateful anything but hurt.

And when she broke under the weight of everything she'd survived, the world pointed at the cracks instead of the hands that caused them.

My mother, Cherry, carried a pain that was never hers to hold. She was taught to smile through it, to make excuses for those who hurt her, to shrink so others could stand taller.

She wasn't just my mother she was my first lesson in what happens when the world punishes a woman for her light. And I saw it every pattern, every silence, every bruise that wasn't visible.

I didn't just inherit her eyes or her laugh I inherited her ghosts.
Every scar they left on me was one I recognized in her.

Writing this book is how I finally stopped mistaking that pain for love.
I wrote this because her story deserved to be told right because so many mothers die unheard, and so many daughters grow up repeating what killed them.

This isn't about revenge it's about release.
It's about freeing both of us from a story that was never ours to carry.

Every chapter in this book is a wound turned into wisdom.
Some pages will ache, because healing always does. But through that ache, there is truth and through truth, there is peace.

I wrote this for anyone who has ever lived inside a family that confuses silence for safety, or love for control.
For anyone who became the reflection of their parents' unhealed pain, and didn't know how to stop the cycle without losing themselves.

This is my stand against the inheritance of trauma against pretending, denying, and swallowing pain until it poisons another generation.

I am here to break it.
For her. For me. For my children.

This is not a story of what broke us.
It's the story of how we're finally free.

Strawberry Wine with Cherry-by Carissa Horton

Prologue
Inheritance of Wings

Generational pain and silence shaped my family.
Every bruise on me once existed in the women before me.
Their stories lived in my skin before I ever understood them.
Their pain became language passed down through looks,
silence, and survival.

I was raised by women who carried storms inside them.
They smiled while bleeding.
They forgave people who never said sorry.
They learned to love from those who mistook control for care.
And I was the child who watched memorizing every kind of ache
until I called it normal.

My mother, Cherry, was both the wound and the remedy.
She gave me the strength to fight and the silence to survive.
She wanted to protect me from the pain she knew too well,
but protection looks different when you're still learning what
peace feels like.

HER LOVE WAS REAL BUT SO WAS HER HURT.

I didn't write this to expose her.
I wrote it to free her.
To give her back the voice the world took away.
To show that even when love comes damaged, it still counts.

The pain that shaped her shaped me too but it ends here.
I am not the silence I inherited.
I am the voice that rises from it.

This book is my Inheritance of Wings
not the kind that fly above the past,
but the kind that carry truth with grace and strength
the kind that rise from the ashes of everything that tried to keep
us grounded.

Chapter 1
-Cherry: The Stolen Glow

To understand the beginning, you must first understand the ending.

When my mother, Cherry, died, I could hardly recognize her. Her body was fragile pale, hollow, almost transparent. She looked worse than any cancer patient, though what had eaten her wasn't illness. It was life itself years of pain and betrayal corroding her from the inside out.

I hadn't seen her in ten years. Ten years of unanswered calls. Ten years of silence and searching. Ten years of wondering whether she was alive somewhere or already gone.

And yet there I was, standing over her deathbed. The woman who had once been a force of light now looked like a ghost of herself. When I looked into her eyes, I knew. She was already gone. Her spirit had died long before her body followed. What remained was only a shell the echo of someone who had spent her whole life giving until there was nothing left to give.

In that moment, I thought Mama, you really did give everything you had.
You gave it to people who took it for granted, to a world that never gave anything back. You gave it to the ones who hurt you, hoping love could save them. And in the end, you gave it to me all the pieces of you that somehow survived.
That's the cruelty of generational trauma it devours the kindest souls first.
It breaks the ones who love the hardest, who forgive the fastest, who never stop hoping that someone will treat them with the same tenderness they've always given away. My mother lived her whole life waiting for safety that never came.

Psychologically, that kind of exhaustion is called spiritual death when the mind and body keep breathing, but the soul stops trying. Trauma doesn't just break hearts it rewires them. It convinces you that surviving is the same as living, and that silence is safer than truth.

Cherry's ending explains her beginning.

The woman who lay in that hospital bed was the same little girl who was never protected, never believed, and never allowed to rest. Her body gave up long after her spirit already had.

One of Cherry's uncles always chose her out of all her sisters. He'd call her to run errands short drives to the store, the kind of small gestures that looked like kindness. But she once told me how he'd make her sit low on the floorboard of the car, how she never understood why only that she felt afraid.

Her childhood ended in that quiet, suffocating fear that had no words.

That's how grooming begins not with violence, but with confusion. It starts with the small choices that isolate a child, the kind of attention that feels special but isn't safe. It teaches them to doubt their instincts, to confuse love with discomfort. Cherry learned that lesson before she even knew what love was.

By the time the older man entered her life, her innocence was already fractured. She was thirteen. He was nearly thirty. People would later whisper the word relationship, but I know the truth it was exploitation wrapped in affection. She had been conditioned to believe that compliance was survival.
And I'll say this no man like that just happens to have access to a household as guarded and controlling as the Monarch of the House was. From a psychological standpoint, I don't believe it could have happened without her knowing. Her need for control was absolute. In families ruled by control, silence becomes complicity. When truth threatens the image, denial becomes the defense. That's.

how abuse hides for generations. The system protects its illusion of order at the expense of its children.

The Monarch of the House her authority depended on keeping secrets, and Cherry's pain became the price of that order. In psychology, this is called protective dissonance when the mind chooses a comforting lie over a destabilizing truth. That's what my family did they preserved their image while my mother unraveled.

Cherry's childhood ended in confusion.
The girl who should have been shielded was instead shamed. They called her "fast," "rebellious," "too much," when in truth, she was a wounded child acting out the only script she'd ever been given.

When she gave birth to a son at fourteen, she thought she had finally done something worthy of love. But the Monarch of the House turned even that into control. The baby became her new obsession the one thing she had always wanted but never had.

The Monarch had given birth to daughters her whole life, but deep down, she wanted a boy. She craved what she believed a son could give her legacy, loyalty, validation. So when Cherry gave birth to a boy, it was as though the Monarch saw her second chance. She didn't see her grandson she saw the son she never had.

And that's when the manipulation began.

She refused to help Cherry unless she surrendered him. She'd say things like, "You can't take care of a baby," or "You don't know what you're doing," while painting herself as the savior. But in truth, she was claiming what she believed was hers.

When the baby became sick, the Monarch wouldn't take him to the hospital until Cherry agreed to hand him over. Eventually, he began calling the Monarch Mom.

That's identity control a psychological way of rewriting family roles to claim ownership over the next generation. It's not love it's possession dressed up as concern.

Once the Monarch had the baby, the dynamic shifted even more. I've often wondered why my mother began spiraling why the partying, the drinking, the drugs took hold when she was still so young. But looking back, I don't think it just happened. I think it was shaped.

From a psychological standpoint, the Monarch didn't just exploit my mother's weaknesses she cultivated them. Control doesn't always come through force sometimes it comes through influence. If you make someone appear unstable, you can justify taking everything from them and still call it help.

I believe the Monarch subtly encouraged my mother's self-destruction not out of hatred, but out of obsession and need for power. She weaponized Cherry's pain to fit the story she needed that my mother was unfit, unreliable, unsafe. The more my mother broke down, the more believable the Monarch's story became.

She became the savior the "responsible one" while my mother became the scapegoat, the chaos that needed to be contained. In psychology, this is called induced dependency when one person keeps another trapped in dysfunction to maintain power. It's gaslighting by design: manipulate someone into appearing unstable, then use their instability as proof of your righteousness.

And it worked.
The family saw Cherry through the Monarch's eyes not as a victim, but as the failure. The more my mother tried to prove her worth, the more the story twisted against her. She wasn't fighting her own choices anymore she was fighting a system built to break her. I wouldn't have died for my mother I would have died because of her. Not from her hands, but from the weight of everything that shaped her. The love I had for her was inseparable from the pain that made her who she was. And in loving her, I was slowly becoming what destroyed her.

Because every ounce of protection she never received, I tried to give her even in her absence. And when the world called her unworthy, I still saw the truth she was a product of manipulation disguised as motherhood, of love turned into leverage.

As she grew older, that pain transformed into addiction, abusive partners, and a constant need to escape her own mind. People saw her as wild, reckless, lost. But I see her differently now. She wasn't lost she was searching. She was chasing the feeling of safety she never got to have.

Addiction wasn't rebellion it was relief. From a psychological perspective, her substance use was an attempt to quiet her trauma response a desperate way to feel in control of a body that had been controlled by others her entire life. Each high numbed the panic each low reminded her that peace was foreign. Her choices weren't about weakness they were about survival.

AND STILL, EVEN THROUGH THE CHAOS, SHE GLOWED.

Cherry had a beauty that no trauma could dull. Auburn hair that caught the light like fire. Green eyes that carried both laughter and sorrow. People said she was too much. But that light the one they tried to dim was the reason I'm still standing today.

In family systems theory, when someone embodies truth inside a family built on secrets, they become the scapegoat. Cherry carried that role long before I was born. She was the family's unspoken shame and its silent truth all at once.

And when I came into the world, mirroring her strength, I inherited that same role. Her trauma became my blueprint. I learned to read moods instead of words, to fix pain that wasn't mine, to stay small so others could stay comfortable. That's what children of trauma do we mistake hyper-vigilance for empathy. It looks like emotional maturity, but it's really survival wearing kindness as armor. When I lost my baby, I finally understood her grief that hollow, unending ache that no one else can touch. But I also found something she never did healing. Her suffering became my map. Psychology became my language for what she endured betrayal trauma, scapegoating, enmeshment, gaslighting, coercive control. Naming them didn't erase the pain, but it freed me from carrying it blindly.

I am my mother's reflection, but I am also her evolution.
Where she stayed silent, I speak.
Where she collapsed, I stand.
Where she lost herself, I am finding both of us.

Breaking the cycle isn't rebellion it's love in its highest form. I don't tell her story to shame her; I tell it so her suffering has meaning. So the world can see what it does to a woman who gives everything and still gets called ungrateful.
Cherry's glow was never just beauty it was resistance.
Even when life stripped her bare, she carried a light that refused to die.She passed it to me the only way she knew how through the cracks.She was their trophy. She was never their favorite and you gotta make your trophy presentable.
"People say my mother was their favorite. But when was that when there was no one else to compare her to, when her beauty still made her a trophy for their stories, or when they ripped her baby from her arms and blamed her for bleeding? or was it conditional just until her beauty faded away??" the answers are there open your eyes!! "The day that truly snapped me open was the day they threatened my motherhood. They tried to sabotage me through my children, to weaponize the very thing that healed me. But they felt the fire that day because I am not my mother, and I am not any of them. I am the evolution of everything they tried to break. And soon, they'll understand the psychology in that."I remember the exact moment I started to feel myself slipping not just mentally, but spiritually. It was when they tried to sabotage me through my children. That was the moment everything in me broke open. It's one thing to destroy a woman, but it's another to weaponize her motherhood against her. That's when the line between reality and manipulation began to blur.

I could feel myself drifting, like my mind was trying to detach to survive. I wasn't crazy I was being cornered. They knew what they were doing. They had already studied my reactions for years, testing the limits of my endurance. And when they saw that love was my strength, they targeted the one thing I loved most.

When someone tries to turn your own children against you, it's not just emotional abuse it's psychological warfare. Every instinct in your body fights to hold on, while your mind starts fragmenting under the weight of disbelief. I was watching my own reality twist in front of me, wondering how people who shared my blood could stoop that low.

That was the moment I realized the system wasn't just external it was inherited. It ran through generations like a poison, and I was the one who had to purge it. I didn't lose my mind that day I was finding it. I was waking up to the truth that my love for my children would be the very thing that saved me from becoming what they wanted me to be.
That's the day I realized I don't Owe these people anything not my silence not their secrets and damn sure not my loyalty.

Her story is my inheritance, but I've rewritten its meaning.
She endured so I could understand.
I understand so I can heal.
And through me, she finally gets to rest.

Chapter 2
— The Family Pattern

Every generation repeats what it refuses to heal. If my mother's life reads like a ledger of survival, this chapter explains the ledger's architecture. Pain in our family had rules, roles, a hierarchy. It had a Monarch. She taught the household a grammar of cruelty, then punished anyone who tried to speak a different language.

THE FIRST WAS THE MONARCH -
 the one who learned control through pain. She was taught that power was safety and that domination was the only way to be untouched. What she didn't understand was that cruelty, once learned, never disappears it simply changes hands.

THE SECOND WAS MY MOTHER -
the one who carried the damage that control left behind. She didn't inherit power she inherited the wound. She kept giving until there was nothing left to give, believing love could heal what obedience never could. It was that belief that relentless faith in people who only knew how to take that slowly killed her.

THE THIRD WAS ME-
the one who saw the pattern for what it was and chose to end it. I broke the cycle not out of anger, but out of love the kind that no longer confuses pain with loyalty. I am the proof that healing can come from ruin.

In our generation it was three. It would have been four if I'd carried it on. The Monarch is sewing the seams again now, raising children who will inherit the same scaffolding but that fourth generation is not mine. I am separate. I severed the line. That separation is the evidence.

The Monarch house was never a home. It was an ecosystem of fear with its own seasons and rituals. Everyone had a role a favorite to validate her capacity to love, a failure to prove punishment had purpose, and onlookers who learned early enough that interfering meant risk. I was the failure the scapegoat, the living demonstration of what happens when you stop obeying.

This is family role conditioning plain and naked. The golden child soaks up praise and safety the scapegoat soaks up blame and ruin. The controller remains untouched. The Monarch called it love clinically, it is coercion disguised as care. That disguise is the engine that preserves the system.

She rationed food the way some people ration forgiveness just enough to keep me alive, never enough to make me feel safe. She handed me scraps from her plate and then named me greedy, fat, ungrateful. Hunger became the first vocabulary of my shame. Deprivation was not an accident it was deliberate pedagogy. In clinical terms it is coercive deprivation using a child's basic needs to teach obedience, to make survival depend on compliance. train me the same way people train a dog.Since I Was a mixed race dealing with racism within my family.
When I asked why I cleaned for ten people and others did nothing, she punished me with isolation. Summers smelled like the back room hot, stale air, sunlight slicing the dust, floorboards keeping time. I measured days by how light moved across the floor. Prolonged isolation paired with starvation rewires a child's sense of safety it breeds learned helplessness the mind stops trying because it expects futility.

When I finally ran for food an act grown of hunger and fear, explained later in this book she threw my belongings over the fence and told me never to come back. That was how my childhood ended not with rescue, but with rejection.
Violence in that house was routine. It organized the day. When I was beaten, faces turned away as if sight could cancel the deed. When I was humiliated, the Monarch scolded witnesses not for hurting me but for letting it be seen. Denial does not erase the act it erases acknowledgement. Silence becomes the currency of loyalty.

Once, I asked why the chores were mine. I was hit until I collapsed. Another adult struck me the Monarch later wrapped a hand around my throat and hissed, "Stop talking about that little girl the favorite." The next day she kissed my forehead in the grocery aisle and told me she loved me. That is manipulation wearing perfume. Psychologists name this trauma bonding cycles of cruelty punctuated by intermittent kindness that root attachment to the abuser. Love becomes a leash.

She weaponized triangulation. By marking one child "good" and another "bad," she turned us into rivals. The favored child learned to protect the image and silence dissent the scapegoat learned that truth equals punishment. Both grew up confusing fear for love. This sibling triangulation is strategy, not accident one of the most effective engines of generational control.

As I grew, the scaffolding revealed itself. The Monarch had been formed by her own wounds she muttered once about being unfed and humiliated by her mother. That's intergenerational trauma transmission pain that is not healed becomes identity. Victimhood, if unprocessed, calcifies into a blueprint for survival later repurposed as domination.

The chain ran forward her mother hurt her she hurt her children her children hurt theirs. I carried the weight of all of it. Family trauma does not live only in memory it lives in tone, in slammed doors, in the way silence settles like dust after an argument. It becomes reaction, ritual, reflex. It passes like an heirloom starvation, shame, silence, rivalry.

Why did I still long for her approval? Because children are wired to bond with caregivers. When abuse mixes with affection, the nervous system bonds to both. That is insecure attachment and trauma reenactment the body repeats what it knows, sometimes hoping this time the wound will close. I defended the Monarch because my early survival responses equated loyalty with safety. What looked like love was conditioning. Her methods were surgical in their mundanity ration the food to teach worth withhold praise to teach dependence stage humiliation to enforce hierarchy offer intermittent rescue to bind loyalties. Praise the golden child to isolate the rest punish one to set the example for all. I learned to read moods instead of words, to smooth myself into tolerable shapes, to make my need small. That is enmeshment the erosion of boundaries where identity is redistributed to uphold the family's secret stability.

There were nights I lay awake and mapped how she parceled out kindness like currency how she taught us to apologize for existing. She taught us etiquette that was survival. She taught us that asking for more was ingratitude. She trained an economy of obedience that looked like love.

I have watched her begin shaping another generation the same way isolating, controlling, whispering that obedience equals safety. The Monarch is building a fourth generation now. She is knitting the same net of cruelty and choosing the same scapegoat. But that fourth generation is not mine. I am separate. I am severed. That distinction is not small it is the proof the pattern can be split.

This is why I write. I remember so it does not remain. Silence is how the pattern survives. Truth is how the Monarch's rule finally ends if noticed.

Read this and do not look away. Let it sit in your chest like a stone. Understand the scaffolding conditioned safety, induced dependency, trauma bonding, coercive deprivation, enmeshment, sibling triangulation, learned helplessness, insecure attachment, trauma reenactment. These are not metaphors. They are methods. They were taught, practiced, and passed down.

If you were raised in a house like that, hear me you are not broken. You were trained to survive. Survival is not shame. The shame belongs to the system that called it love.

If you are someone who continues to call a hand that hurt you "mother," look at the architecture. Look at the labor of the methods. See the deliberate economy of control. Let that recognition be the first step out.

I am writing this not to indict every woman who raised me, but to strip the world's language of its excuses. This is to dismantle an empire of secrecy by naming its tools. I broke the pattern. I learned to separate need from obligation, love from leverage. I learned to protect what is mine without becoming what hurt me.

Breaking a lineage of harm is brutal and merciful. It is a defiant love.

So when you finish this, do not let it be something you glance at and set down. Let it alter the way you see small cruelties the rationed forgiveness, the loyalty enforced like law, jokes that humiliate disguised as "tough love." Name them. Stop them.

BECAUSE SILENCE IS THE MONARCH'S ALLY. TRUTH IS THE LAST LIGHT THAT CAN UNMAKE HER.

Chapter 3
— Before the Separation

Before the system ever stepped in, I had already been taken five times.
Four of those times ended the same way returned to the Monarch's care as if abuse were gravity.
But the fifth time was different.
She didn't want me back.

NOT BECAUSE SHE HAD CHANGED.
Not because anyone finally believed me.
But because she had lost control of me.
And once she couldn't control me, I stopped being valuable to her.
Her love had always been a transaction built on power.
When obedience ran out, so did affection.
To her, losing control wasn't losing a child it was losing possession.

People sensed something in her, though they couldn't name it.
Visitors felt the air change on her porch neighbors crossed the street.
Strangers described a chill they couldn't explain.
But the professionals missed it the way they always miss the quiet kinds of evil that hide behind tidy houses and polite smiles.

They missed it because they were trained to measure harm by injury instead of impact.
Because the Monarch knew how to bruise without leaving marks.
Because she used words as weapons and silence as proof of control.
She could cry on command, speak about "misunderstood children," and charm the very people who were supposed to see through her.

Professionals miss predators like her because they expect monsters to look monstrous.
They don't expect them to stand in a doorway pretending affection while the truth hides behind the walls.
If a real professional had ever stepped past the threshold and actually looked, they couldn't have missed it.
There was the "children's room," spotless and staged for display but whose room was it, really?
There were toys lined neatly on shelves, yet none of them were mine.
There were soft blankets folded for show, but on the other side of the hallway was the place that smelled of dog urine and mildew, the place where I slept.
They could have followed the stains, the cracked plaster, the scar that ran across my forehead and asked how it got there.
They could have noticed that the child they were told was "well-fed" had a swollen belly from malnutrition.
They could have asked why a little girl who supposedly ate too much at school was also eating from the trash behind the cafeteria.
Every answer was visible in plain sight.
They simply never looked long enough to connect it.

The Monarch didn't hide her cruelty she curated it.
She built a display of "motherhood" around her favorite child the proof she offered to the world that she could love.
The rest of us were props to keep that image believable.
And that is what reveals the truth if she could fool them so completely, then she always knew exactly what she was doing.
That doesn't make her broken it makes her intentional.
It makes her cruel.

They don't recognize coercive control when it's wrapped in domestic normalcy.
They saw a well-dressed woman with a rehearsed story and a quiet house.
They saw children who didn't cry in front of strangers and thought that meant peace.
They never asked why we were so calm, why our voices shook, why we looked at the floor when she spoke.
They didn't understand that stillness in children can be a trauma response that it's what happens when fear teaches you that movement invites danger.

The professionals missed it because the signs weren't loud.
They were subtle, psychological, and buried under years of conditioning.
They missed it because they only checked our skin when the damage lived in our nervous systems.

It was the kind of harm that doesn't leave clean scars.
It hides beneath the skin, waits in the nervous system, and teaches the body to brace for storms that never stop coming.
My body learned chaos as normal.
I became fluent in survival long before I knew what safety meant.

This is where you can hold someone accountable for the trauma they pass down. Every person who reflected the Monarch's shadow continued to spread the lies, to scapegoat, to hurt the reflection they saw in me all to stay comfortable in their own denial. Each one of them passed down their pain.

But my mother… my mother was different. She was the only one who truly believed that love could save them. That's why she wasn't a monster. That's why I don't blame her.

But I do blame the Monarch. Because everything written in this book and everything I've come to understand points to one truth she knew what she was doing. She chose to continue the generational abuse. She knew it was wrong that's why she hid it from the social workers. She knew it was wrong that's why she kept me home from school when the bruises became visible.

People subconsciously pass down trauma without realizing it and that's one thing. But when you know what you're doing, when you know it's wrong and still choose to do it, that's when you become the problem. That's when you're wrong.

In that house, pain came before understanding and silence came before words.
My earliest memories are stitched with hunger and noise doors slamming, voices colliding, my name used as an accusation.
The air thickened before anyone spoke.
My body always knew before my mind did something bad was coming.
That instinct, later, would have a name hyper-vigilance but at the time it was simply breath held too long.

There's one memory that never fades.
I was small enough to believe adults existed to protect.
Instead, I became their release valve the place where their anger landed when it couldn't land anywhere else.
When hands came down, they didn't just bruise they rewired the way I interpreted the world.
Every strike told my brain anticipate pain, even in peace.

Blows to my head left more than marks.
They changed how sound became meaning.
Years later doctors would call it Auditory Processing Disorder, this is a condition that professional boxers deal with from blows to their head but as a child it just felt like noise turning to fog words dissolving before I could catch them.

Behind the house was a patch of dirt near the back fence.
That's where I sat when I was locked out or too afraid to go back in.
I stared at the gate and wondered if the world outside could ever be different.
But when you grow up in isolation, even freedom feels dangerous.
Outside doesn't promise safety it only promises unknown.

Hunger was constant not the kind that fades, but the kind that fuses with identity.
It hurts more in the chest than the stomach.
I watched plates I wasn't allowed to touch, watched others eat while I swallowed air and guilt.
I was told I didn't deserve more.
That's what coercive deprivation does it teaches a child that nourishment must be earned, that worth is rationed.
It seeps into everything relationships, self-esteem, even breathing.

The night that shaped me most began when she kicked me outside to sleep in a plastic playhouse.
The air was sharp, the walls warm from the day's sun, smelling of dust and grass.
Three adults stood at the window and watched.
They whispered that it was wrong, but not one opened the door.
That is what collective trauma looks like everyone sees, no one acts.

I remember sitting on the ground, the world holding its breath.
A belt lay half-buried in the dirt the same one that had struck me before.
I picked it up, thinking maybe it would hurt less if I was the one holding it.
I was eight years old, and the thought that came wasn't childish it was final.

That's what trauma does to children it teaches death as a kind of rest.
When a home is ruled by fear, the idea of stopping the pain can feel like safety.

I didn't die that night, but something inside me did.
The part that believed help would come.
The part that still hoped.

Looking back, the separation didn't begin when CPS removed me it began that night in the yard when love turned into something I had to earn.
It began the first time I went to bed hungry and decided it was my fault.
It began the first time I learned to cry quietly because loud crying only made things worse.

That's the cruelty of childhood trauma it convinces you that you are the reason you're unloved.

The theme of those years was simple damage started before language.
I didn't have words, only sensations hunger, fear, silence.
My body spoke long before I did.

And that's what people still misunderstand about children raised in chaos.
They don't act out because they're bad they react because their bodies are permanently on alert.
They don't rebel they defend.

By the time I was finally removed, there wasn't much left to rescue.
The belief in safety was already gone.

Yet even then, something in me chose to live.
Even then, the story was already bending toward survival

Chapter 4 —
The Attempt at Age Twelve

By twelve, I already knew what violence looked like in my family, but I didn't yet know how far it could go.
Before more girls were born before I was five I remember being treated differently.
They dressed me in matching clothes, sometimes even new.
I was the first girl of our generation.
So was my mother.
So was the Monarch.
So was the Monarch's mother.
That's the cycle the eldest, the strongest, the most aware becomes the target.

At first, there was no one to compare me to no one else to project on.
It wasn't love it was convenience.
I was too small to threaten anyone yet.
But as more girls arrived, the hierarchy shifted.
Their smiles earned praise my presence earned criticism.
In that house, affection was rationed like food a psychological currency given only when it reinforced control.

By grade school, birthdays stopped.
School clothes vanished.
At first, she bought them for show, but as time passed, even that performance faded.
Another adult in the household began taking the few hand-me-downs I owned shirts, pants, shoes the tiny things that reminded me I still existed.
I kept them folded in one small cabinet, my secret world inside a house that wasn't safe.

When I took them back quietly, folding each piece like a prayer another adult in the household came for me.
She moved too fast for me to scream.
Her hand gripped my hair and slammed my head against the pool table.

The crack sounded before pain arrived.
Blood ran down my face, hot and metallic, and I thought so this is what love looks like here.

THE MONARCH DIDN'T HAVE TO THROW THE PUNCHES.
She had already built the system that would.
That's how generational control works it delegates the violence so the Monarch's image stays clean while her influence remains absolute.
The hands that hurt me weren't acting alone they were carrying out a script she had written long before I was born.
That's what makes her power so insidious she could watch cruelty unfold and still look like the savior.
That's how she stayed clean while the damage multiplied.

Then came her hands around my throat.
Not wild precise.
Both thumbs pressed beneath my jaw, where breath begins.
My vision blurred, sound drained away, the world tilted.
My mind split in two one part gasping, the other floating above, watching.
That's dissociation the brain's last defense when the body believes it's dying.

She didn't stop from guilt she stopped because she remembered consequences.
When she released me, I collapsed to the floor, lungs clawing for air that tasted like metal and dust.
Psychologically, that moment became the blueprint for every reaction afterward.
It's how complex trauma imprints itself the nervous system forever braced for an ending that never quite arrives.

I stumbled outside, barefoot and bleeding.
A police officer found me wandering the road.
He asked what happened.
I tried to answer, but my throat burned where her hands had been.

Silence came easier.
Silence felt safer.
So when he asked if everything was okay, I nodded.
That's what trauma teaches children to lie convincingly enough to survive.

He drove me back to the same house.
She waited on the porch, already performing worry.
The officer believed her.
They always did.
Evil like hers survives through performance, not power.

Later that same day, she came for me again outside this time.
When the Monarch's car appeared, the rage turned theatrical.
She began screaming louder, thrashing as though I were attacking her.
That was the lesson control the narrative and you never need to control your actions.
By the time my bruises darkened, the story had already been rewritten.

They still tell it that way that I attacked her.
They leave out the crack of skull against wood, the fingers around my throat, the blood in my mouth.
That's what betrayal feels like not just pain, but erasure.
It's watching the person who almost killed you walk away as the victim while you are forced to stay quiet.

She beat me the rest of that day.
Violence was no longer punishment it was reinforcement.
In trauma psychology, that's called conditioning repetition that rewires the brain to expect pain as proof of belonging.
After enough cycles, the child stops resisting survival becomes compliance.
That's how the mind protects itself by turning surrender into safety, silence into love.
It's the cruelest defense mechanism of all, because once the body learns to submit, it doesn't know how to stop.

"The adult household member wasn't just trying to kill me she was trying to destroy the reflection of what I meant to her.I didn't write everyone's story in that house, because their trauma isn't mine to tell. But what I will say is this I was her reflection. I mirrored the very pain they endured, the innocence they lost, and the parts of themselves they buried. And that's why they became the monster that once hurt them because I reminded them of everything they could never heal."

That's what happened to my mother, Cherry.
She lived her entire life in that mode compliance mistaken for peace, obedience mistaken for worth.
Her nervous system never unlicked from survival.
Even when there were no hands around her throat, she still flinched like there were.
Cherry's heart kept beating long after her spirit had already shut down.
That's what killed her long before her body followed she couldn't turn off the part of herself that believed silence could save her.
She didn't die of weakness she died of endurance.

My mother had nowhere else to go.
From early childhood, the Monarch's house was all she knew a place that stripped her of everything, including her own baby.
Later, she stayed there, trapped between motherhood and captivity, forced to watch the Monarch raise me as if I were hers.
Even if Cherry wanted to do it herself, it was impossible.
We already learned that lesson earlier in this story in that house, control was disguised as care.
Leaving wasn't abandonment it was mercy.
For her, it was easier to be gone than to keep breathing inside a cage that called itself family.

At five, I was already cleaning for ten people changing diapers, cooking, babysitting toddlers while being scolded for every imperfection.
That's role reversal, when a child becomes the caretaker to appease unstable adults.
It steals innocence and replaces it with exhaustion mistaken for maturity.

I wasn't allowed to do homework.
They said I was pretending.
At school I was called names, marked as a problem.
That's how systemic neglect hides by mislabeling trauma responses as attitude.
Teachers saw behavior they never saw the bruises that lived under obedience.

I slept on the floor where the dogs relieved themselves.
One thin blanket stiff with bleach, smelling of dirt separated me from the concrete.
That's coercive degradation stripping comfort to redefine worth.
After a while, my body believed that filth was home and rest was a luxury I hadn't earned.

Once, the Monarch received a child-support check from my father.
I asked if I could have shoes for school.
She said, "That money isn't yours. It's mine for taking care of you."
That single sentence teaches transactional love the belief that care must be purchased with obedience.

Another time I snuck a bowl of cereal because I was hungry.
She caught me and said, "That cereal's for the kids."
I was twelve.
That's how neglect speaks by rewriting reality so the victim doesn't qualify as human.

The smallest wound came at five.
I looked in the mirror and whispered, You're so beautiful, Carissa.
The Monarch walked by, paused, and said, "No, you're not. You don't look like the other little girls." They where white enough not me so to them I wasn't beautiful. My oldest brother, looked indigenous but it was an exception because he was a boy. That's self-concept sabotage extinguishing self-love before it can threaten control.
From then on, every compliment felt dangerous. There was always money for casinos, never for me.
The favorite child had everything new I had rags and chores.
One day we watched old home videos recorded by another adult. I was in the background small, silent until her voice cut through, screaming, hitting, calling me names.
Seeing it later confirmed what memory alone couldn't prove.
I wasn't exaggerating.
I was documented.
I had lived through hell, and someone filmed it.

That footage still exists.
It's proof that cruelty was not a story I invented it was a system everyone saw and chose not to stop.

If I could speak to the one who wrapped her hands around my throat, I'd ask
Were those clothes really worth it?
You broke my head open over shirts I folded back into a cabinet.
You strangled me for claiming a corner of space that belonged to no one.
And then you rewrote it so the world would pity you.
You walk through life pretending it never happened, but you'll die knowing I remember every second you tried to take my breath.

That was the day the child in me died and the survivor was born.
The innocence that believed in rescue dissolved, replaced by the cold understanding that I would have to become my own protection.
No one apologized.
No one admitted what they'd done.
But my body kept the record the tension in my neck, the fear at

raised voices, the silence that feels like safety
When people ask what betrayal feels like, I don't describe pain.
I describe revision.
The rewriting of truth until you start doubting your own memory.
The eyes that watched and did nothing.
The child who folded her shirts like evidence and prayed someone would notice.

If this chapter leaves you with one truth, let it be this:
Cruelty like that isn't confusion.
It's design.
And the only way to end a design like that is to expose exactly how it was built
so no one else ever has to live inside it again.

Chapter 5
— When She Saw

To understand my mother's pain, you have to see the moment she tried to come back.

I was six years old, sitting in the bathtub with my cousin. It was innocent two little girls playing in the water, laughing in the only way children know how. But in a house built on suspicion and shame, innocence was never safe for long.

Another household member walked in, saw what she wanted to see, and turned that moment into something ugly. Before I could even understand what she was angry about, she called for the Monarch, yanked me out of the bathtub, water spilling across the floor. She beat me while I was still wet her hands sharp and cold, her voice filled with disgust. Then she left me there crying, trembling, and exposed on the cold tile.

That's when my mother walked in.
They didn't know she was there.
The Monarch had no idea that Cherry the daughter she had shamed, abandoned, and punished was standing in her house again, hearing everything.

My mother came into the room quietly. When she saw me, her face changed. I don't think I'll ever forget the look in her eyes the

pain, the disbelief, the guilt. She rushed over, grabbed a towel, and wrapped me in it like she was trying to erase every bruise that came before. She pulled me close, carried me to the front room, and held me against her chest.

She whispered questions through tears, her voice shaking. I leaned in close and told her the truth
"I'm hungry."

I told her they hadn't fed me in a long time.
She didn't speak for a while. She just held me tighter, her arms trembling, her breath uneven. Then she dressed me in silence, took my hand, and we left.

Later, they said she kidnapped me.
But the Monarch never called the police because she knew my mother had every right to take her child.

We ended up at a small motel on a busy road where people came and went for reasons no child should understand. The walls were thin, the lights flickered, and the air smelled like cigarettes and rain. But for the first time in my life, I felt peace.

At night, my mother held me so close I could feel her heartbeat in my ear. She kissed the top of my head, whispered prayers she barely believed in, and said, "You're safe now, baby. I've got you. Nobody's going to hurt you again."

One night, I overheard her talking to someone outside the bathroom. Her voice was low but full of fire. She said, "The Monarch used to starve my sister like that. She was the target. And now she's doing it to Carissa. I see it now and I'm not going to let it happen."

That was the moment my mother saw it all the same cruelty that had shaped her childhood was now reaching for me. Psychologically, that's called generational recognition the moment a survivor finally sees the pattern they once endured reflected in their own child. It isn't just awareness. It's a breaking point the instant the heart can no longer lie to itself.

My mother tried to protect me the only way she knew how. She had no resources, no home, no support. The world had taught her since she was thirteen that her body was her only form of currency. So she used it not out of choice, but desperation.

During the day, she met men to keep food in our stomachs and a roof over our heads. At night, she came back to me tired, fragile, but alive. She would hold me close, stroke my hair, and whisper, "You're not like them. You're going to have a better life."

And I believed her.
She was far from perfect, but in that small, flickering motel room, I felt a kind of love that was real not clean, not polished, but raw and desperate and true.

One day, while she was in the bathroom, one of the Monarch's old friends came to the door. I do believe this person was having relations with my mother in exchange for money. I didn't know him well, but he had been around before. He took me while she was inside. I don't remember everything that happened only the feeling the cold rush of fear, the silence in my chest, the sense that something terrible had just begun.

When I saw one of the old household members walking up with the Monarch later that day, I froze. My stomach twisted. My mother panicked when she realized I was gone. That night, she came back for me again right in front of them. I still remember their faces shock, disbelief. She took me back to that motel.

SHE WASN'T GIVING UP ON ME.

We stayed there for another month. Despite the chaos, despite everything happening around us, it was one of the happiest times of my childhood. She bought me food. She brushed my hair. She told me I was beautiful. For once, I wasn't invisible.

Then one morning, I woke up to the sound of unfamiliar voices.
Child Protective Services had come.
It wasn't a coincidence. It was a setup.
A household member from that house had called them not because they loved me, but because they wanted me.
They wanted control.
And they knew exactly how to get it.
They knew CPS would come, find my mother, and see only the

drugs not the woman, not the truth, not the reason behind her desperation.
They knew the system would do what they couldn't label her as broken, unfit, unstable.
And it worked.
CPS didn't come that day to protect a child.
They came to reinforce a story one written long before I was even born.

I opened my eyes and saw my mother sitting on the edge of the bed, her face pale, her hands trembling. She didn't fight. She didn't yell. She just sat there, tears rolling silently down her cheeks. I think she already knew what was happening.

When you are a child so closely connected to your parent, especially the way me and my mother were, you can feel the brokenness in them. You can feel the emptiness, especially when you're being separated. She knew that if she told the truth if she told them what her mother really was they'd never let her see me again.

So she stayed silent. That was the only power she had left to choose how she lost me.

In her mind, sending me back to that house meant she might still be able to find me someday. It was her way of keeping the door open, even if it meant breaking her own heart.

Psychologically, that's what trauma does to a mother. It teaches her that love and sacrifice are the same thing. It convinces her that saving her child might mean losing them.

A few months later, she showed up again. It was summer the kind of heat that makes the pavement shimmer. She came with a small bag of fireworks and a spark in her eyes a glimpse of the woman she once was before the world broke her.

When I saw her, I ran straight into her arms. She smelled like cigarettes and cheap vanilla perfume the scent that still lives in my memory, sweet and heavy, like she was trying to mask the pain the world made her carry. To me, that smell meant love.

We went outside in the front yard. She lit sparklers and handed one to me, showing me how to wave it slow enough to make light trails in the air. For a while, it was just laughter the sound of a little girl and her mother sharing something pure.

Then a firework tipped over. It sparked too close, burning against my skin. I cried out from the sting, startled and scared. My mother dropped to her knees, pulled me into her arms, and whispered, "You're okay, baby. I've got you." She brushed my hair back, blew on the burn, and held me close.

That's when the front door flew open.
The Monarch and another household member stormed outside, voices sharp and cutting through the night. The other woman shouted that my mother needed to "stop babying her," to "quit treating her like she's special."

I can still see my mother's face confusion, then pain. She didn't understand why comforting her hurt child was something to be punished for. But I do now.

Psychologically, that was the moment the cycle exposed itself again love being shamed, tenderness being seen as weakness. In families ruled by control, affection becomes rebellion.

My mother's gentleness challenged the system. Because if love could exist openly, then the entire foundation of fear would crumble.
That's what they were afraid of. Not the fireworks. Not the noise. But the sight of a mother finally loving the daughter they had spent years trying to destroy.

She took me again that night.
She knew she'd have to bring me back, but it was her small escape.

We had no money for the motel room. The owner's knock came like a final sentence dull, inevitable. My mother didn't argue she just nodded, held my hand tighter, and walked us back into the night. The plastic grocery bag she carried rustled with every step, filled with all that was left of our lives.

We walked down the main road the one I knew too well. The same road where the streetlights buzzed like tired angels. The same road where men slowed their cars and pointed, sometimes at her, sometimes at me. The same road where childhood was something that lived in other people's homes.

It smelled like cigarettes, sweat, and survival. Every corner held a story I was too young to hear and too old to forget. My mother's palm was clammy against mine, her nails bitten down, her movements jittery with exhaustion. But she kept walking, like the world owed her a destination.

A few blocks down stood a line of abandoned trailers hollow bones of forgotten lives. She pushed open a door and led me inside. The air was thick with mildew and rust. The floor was cold and damp, and when I sat down, it bit into my skin.

She lay beside me, pulling me against her chest. Her heartbeat was wild uneven, frightened, alive. She smelled of cheap vanilla perfume and cigarette smoke the scent of someone trying to mask pain with memory. I pressed my face into her and inhaled everything I could before the world took it away.

Outside, sirens moaned somewhere in the distance. Inside, there was only her voice.

She whispered,
"It won't always be like this, baby. One day, I'm gonna give you your own room."

Then she started to describe it soft pink walls, lace curtains that fluttered when the window was open, a little lamp beside the bed that made the room glow like sunrise, a doll waiting on the pillow.

She was painting something sacred out of nothing building safety with her words because the world had given her none.

I didn't understand then, but I do now.
That was her way of protecting me constructing safety through vision when reality offered none.
When trauma steals a mother's power to provide, imagination becomes resistance.
She couldn't give me shelter, so she gave me a dream.

And sometimes, a dream is the only thing that keeps a child alive.

Even my mother knew then despite CPS already taking me away, despite the world deciding that she was too broken to be trusted she came anyway, found me anyway, even if it was too late by everyone else's rules. She was late, yes but she came.

That night, lying on that cold floor beside her, I realized something that I've carried my whole life
Being there with her broken, trembling, starving was still better than what I had to go back to.

Because in her chaos, she still loved me in a way no one else ever did. She saw me.

The system never understood that. They saw her addiction, her instability, her shaking hands but I saw the way she still tried. The way she held me tighter when I cried. The way she whispered promises into the dark, even when she had nothing left.

Her body was alive, but her spirit was already fading. I didn't know it then, but I was lying beside a woman who had already given everything she had to a world that never gave her anything back.

Years later, I built that room myself for my daughter.
Pink walls. Lace curtains. A warm lamp by the bed. A doll waiting on the blanket.

Every time I step into that room, I feel my mother's presence not as she was in that trailer, but as she wanted to be. Free. Soft. Whole.

That room isn't just decoration. It's redemption.
It's the dream my mother built with her voice and that I finished with my hands.
It's proof that even the most broken love can plant something sacred that blooms long after the person who planted it is gone.

That room is where my mother lives now not in ashes, not in pain but in the gentle sunlight spilling through lace curtains, in the soft hum of safety she once imagined for me, and that I finally created for her.

THE GRAND-DAUGHTER WHO GOT THE ROOM.

Chapter 6
— The Day She Came Back for Me

Time went on.
I was a little older when my mother came back for me. After years of being taken and returned by CPS like a misplaced package, she appeared one morning at my school as if no time had passed. Calm. Focused. Determined. She told them she was there to pick up her daughter.

When she reached for my hand, I didn't hesitate.
SHE DIDN'T STEAL ME.
SHE SAVED ME.

Her boyfriend waited outside in the car. As we drove away, I stared out the window at the house that had starved me and called it love. For the first time, I wasn't scared of what came next. For a little while, I had a mother again. She brushed my hair, packed my lunches, tied my shoes, and told me I was beautiful. For the first time again, I felt seen. I felt like someone's child.

But trauma doesn't vanish just because life starts to look normal. It waits silent, patient until the world slows down enough to return.
Her boyfriend was cruel. His words cut her down piece by piece until she began to believe them. I saw it happen in real time the way her shoulders drooped, her laughter shortened, her eyes started to fade. The same light that once radiated from her began to flicker.

Then came the whispers.
At first, she murmured softly to herself, sentences too quiet to understand. Then the voices multiplied faster, overlapping, louder Until it felt like she was living in two worlds at once.

I didn't understand what was happening. I only knew I was watching my mother slip away.

Years later, I would learn the word for it schizophrenia.
But clinical terms never capture the horror of watching someone's mind fracture. Schizophrenia isn't just a diagnosis it's the brain's last, desperate attempt to survive what the soul can't bear to process. When trauma piles too high, the mind splits reality in two one world to live in, one world to hide in. My mother's mind wasn't betraying her. It was protecting her the only way it knew how.

Some nights she cried for no reason, rocking herself in the dark. Other nights she hummed lullabies to no one. Sometimes she would hold me close and whisper, "I don't want to be like them."
And then came the pills.
So many pills.

One night she took too many. I remember the sound of her body hitting the floor, the metallic clang of dropped medication bottles, the paramedics pushing a tube down her throat as she thrashed. She wasn't fighting them because she wanted to die. She was fighting because she no longer remembered how to live. I didn't cry. I just stood there frozen. Because deep down, I already knew what I was witnessing the exact moment when someone's spirit starts to leave their body before death ever claims it.

She survived.
But every return took more of her with it. Her voice grew smaller, her hands trembled as she brushed my hair and asked about school. The hospitals became routine she'd vanish for weeks at a time, then come home pretending nothing happened.
I loved her for trying. Even when her mind drifted far from me, she fought to stay my mother.

Then the world turned again. Her boyfriend convinced her to apply for disability in my name. That's when the real distortion began when she started telling doctors that I was unstable, I was out of control.

I wasn't.
I was a quiet little girl living inside her storm.

But the doctors didn't see that. They didn't look at the trembling hands or the vacant eyes of the woman sitting beside me. They saw her confidence and my silence, and they mistook it for truth. They wrote their notes, signed their papers, and handed me a diagnosis that wasn't mine.

They gave me a big yellow pill that made me sleep through entire days.

Transference Trauma

Now I understand.
What happened to me has a name transference trauma when a parent unconsciously projects their unresolved pain onto their child. In psychology, this is called projective identification the parent places the unbearable parts of themselves into the child and then relates to the child as if those parts truly belong to them.
It's not malice. It's survival.
She wasn't trying to hurt me she was trying to stay alive by splitting her pain across two bodies.

But that's how the system fails people like her. The doctors didn't question her story because she was articulate enough to sound credible and broken enough to seem sympathetic.
When clinicians overlook the source of symptoms, they end up treating the echo.
And I became that echo.

They medicated me for her hallucinations.
They labeled me with her despair.
They silenced me with the same pills that numbed her.

That's how trauma replicates itself in a lineage not through blood, but through misunderstanding.

The Disappearance

Her mind continued to unravel.
Her voice slipped into languages I didn't recognize. Her eyes stared at corners of the room where nothing moved.
The woman who once held me and promised me safety now rocked in the dark, whispering to ghosts I couldn't see. Her body remained, but her soul was already half gone.

When CPS came again, she didn't fight. She just looked at me and said, "I love you. I don't wanna send you back. But they are." And she was right.

They took me back to the Monarchs' house the same house that had broken her long before it broke me.

The Collapse

A year later, her boyfriend's mother came for me again. She said my mother wanted me home. I didn't believe her until I saw her thin, pale, fragile, but smiling. For a moment, the light returned. She brushed my hair again, called me beautiful again, and for a brief, impossible second, I felt like we might be okay.

But hope is fragile when the brain is at war with itself. Her overdoses became more frequent, her hospital stays shorter. Her mind and body were collapsing under decades of cumulative trauma.
Psychologists call it cumulative trauma collapse when the human psyche has endured so much sustained stress that its capacity

for recovery simply shuts down. It isn't weakness it's exhaustion on a cellular level.
Her neurons were drowning in memory. Her body remembered every beating, every abandonment, every betrayal. And there is only so much a nervous system can take before it starts to break in self-defense.

Eventually, CPS came for the last time. They said she could no longer care for me at all. I was placed once more back into the Monarchs' house the birthplace of every wound we shared.

That was the end of that chapter of hope.
The little safety she had built for us collapsed like a house of cards. But even in madness, she never stopped being my mother.

**Her mind broke because
she had been strong for too long.
Her illness wasn't weakness
it was the cost of survival.
And though schizophrenia took her far from me, her love never left.**

Even when her mind let go, her heart never did.

Chapter 7
— The Month of Hunger

The Monarch moved us into a small house across the street from a pink liquor store.
I never went inside. I wasn't curious about anything anymore.

Nobody took pictures of me because nobody cared whether I was there. I wasn't going to school. I had no hygiene products, no clothes that fit, and no baby photos to prove I'd ever been someone's child. What little I owned disappeared into adult hands and hands trembling from withdrawal, hands thin enough to fit into a twelve-year-old's clothes until the word mine stopped meaning anything. years later, a third-party had a picture.
Most days I cleaned for ten people, changed other people's children, and took blame for the filth they refused to see. I felt less than human.
I felt like furniture.

THE BEATING

One day, I left. I shouldn't have, but I did.
A friend was having a birthday party laughter, cake, a normal day in someone else's life. I remember eating and thinking it was the first real food I'd had in weeks.

When I came home, my grandfather was waiting.
He beat me so hard the world went silent. His fists met my face, his weight crushed the air from my lungs. When it was over, my shoes were still standing where I had been, untouched as if even they refused to see.

Some relatives still laugh about that night. They tell it like a story, like it's funny that a grown man beat a child half to death.
That's what denial does it turns violence into entertainment so no one has to face what it really was.

After that, something in me shut off.
I stopped cleaning. I stopped obeying.
And that's when she turned on me.

THE LOCK AND THE ROOM

The Monarch locked me in the small back room a space barely larger than a closet, wedged between the house and the yard.
The door to the house was locked tight. The back door stayed cracked not locked, not welcoming just a reminder that escape existed, but safety didn't.

At first she came every few days, shouting through the door, striking me when she opened it. One day, she slapped me across the face. I saw white, then red, then rage. And for the first time, I hit her back.

That moment changed everything.
Her face went blank not surprised, but offended, as if I had broken an unspoken rule only she could cause pain.
When it ended, her eyes burned with hate. I knew I'd crossed a line I would never be forgiven for.

After that, she told the story differently. She called one of the others and said I had "gone crazy." They believed her because it was easier than remembering their own bruises.
That's how family systems like ours survive by recycling pain and calling it discipline.

Then she stopped feeding me.

STARVATION-CONTROL AND COLLAPSE

Days blurred. My stomach twisted into knots so tight I could hear them. I drank water from the bathroom sink when she forgot to lock the door. When she didn't, I drank from the yard.

Starvation isn't just hunger; it's humiliation turned inward.
It's the weaponization of need control in its purest form, where the body betrays the soul.

Psychologically, deprivation rewires the mind. The brain enters survival cognition, where every thought narrows to a single purpose submission equals food.
Hunger teaches obedience better than fear ever could.

I began sneaking out through the back door whenever I could.
I'd wander across the neighborhood searching for my mother.
Sometimes I'd find her. She'd give me a sandwich, a dollar, a hug and I'd go back.
People would later ask why I ate so slowly, why I seemed afraid to eat.
I wasn't embarrassed.
I was remembering what it felt like to be punished for being hungry.

Then one day, when I came back, both doors were locked.
The house door. The yard door.
Everything sealed.

My few things the blanket, the small pile of clothes, the last proof I existed in that house were inside. She kept them. And shut me out.

OUTSIDE

I stayed outside.
Night after night, I walked the streets because it felt safer than closing my eyes.
I didn't sleep. I walked until my legs shook, until exhaustion replaced thought. Sometimes I collapsed, slipped into unconsciousness, and woke up not knowing where I was.

At thirteen, that was survival not hope, not rescue, just movement.
Motion was the only thing that proved I was still alive.

Eventually, I found my mother again. She was staying with her boyfriend, and she let me stay there too. For two months, I had a bed again or something like it.
But the world wasn't done. Violence found me again in that house. Her boyfriend crossed a boundary that could never be uncrossed.

The police were called. They asked The Monarch if she would take me back.
She said no.
She told them I was "too much trouble."

I wasn't too much.
I just wasn't controllable anymore and without control, I wasn't valuable.

To the system, I was a neglected child.
To me, I was the consequence of deliberate cruelty.

No one ever told them about the back room, the month without food, or the girl who stayed awake until her body forgot how to rest.

That month of hunger became my blueprint for strength.
It taught me what silence feels like inside the body.
It taught me that exhaustion becomes memory's shadow.
And that sometimes, survival isn't pretty it's defiant.

AFTERMATH-THE SYSTEM

I entered foster care at thirteen. Between thirteen and seventeen, I moved through more than forty foster homes and three group homes.

At first, I lost track.
The faces blurred. The walls changed, but the cold stayed the same.
Some homes offered food but no warmth. Others gave rules but no love. Most were in it for the check.

In some homes, I was abused. In others, I saw things no child should ever see.
One group home had no furniture just bare mattresses on the floor, white walls, and silence that echoed like punishment.
It felt like jail, even though I hadn't done anything wrong.

In my very last foster home, I kicked down the door to my foster sister's room after she hung herself. I felt it before it happened the stillness, the shift in air.
For years after, I'd imagine doing the same.
Psychologically, that's what trauma does it bonds you to death through familiarity.
When pain becomes predictable, it starts to feel like safety.

And when despair is all you've known, survival starts to feel like betrayal.

After about a year, they sent me back to The Monarch, back into the same hands that had starved me.
It was a different house, but the same sickness lived there.
She didn't get me back because she loved me.
She got me back because the check was bigger.

I didn't stay long.
By fourteen, I ran away again.
For a year, San Francisco became both my battlefield and my refuge.
I learned the streets before I ever learned love.
Freedom wasn't soft or safe   it was cold, loud, and lonely.
But it was mine.

THAT YEAR CHANGED EVERYTHING.

Chapter 8
— The Streets Taught Me

The foster homes were never really homes.
I was just another kid they got paid to keep alive, and even that part felt optional.

Every single one of them had food in the fridge I wasn't allowed to touch.
I'd watch them feed their kids while I sat there hungry, pretending I wasn't.
They told me to wait for my clothing allowance, but half the time it never came.
By the time they remembered, my shoes had holes, my pants didn't fit, and I'd already planned my next run.

The system didn't care if I froze or starved as long as I stayed quiet.
So I stopped waiting.
Every time it got bad, I ran.

People call that "running away," like it's rebellion.
It wasn't.
IT WAS SURVIVAL.

THE PSYCHOLOGY OF RUNNING

When you grow up in chaos, your body learns that stillness is dangerous.
Calm means something is coming. Silence means someone's about to break it.
That's what trauma conditioning does it trains the nervous system to treat safety as a lie.

So when a foster parent raised their voice, my body didn't wait to hear why.
My brain didn't process tone it processed threat.
I wasn't running from them I was running from her, from The Monarch, from every locked room and clenched jaw that ever promised "this is for your own good."

Psychologists call it trauma reactivation when the present becomes contaminated by the past.
Every home that was supposed to protect me triggered the memory of one that didn't.
Every hand that reached too quickly made my lungs forget how to breathe.
Every closed door reminded me how hunger sounds in the dark.

So I ran.
Not because I wanted to escape the world but because I wanted to escape memory.

THE STREETS-HONEST PAIN

I felt more human sleeping on the streets than I ever did under anyone's roof.
At least out there, nobody lied to me.
Hunger on the streets was honest.
Cold nights didn't pretend to love you.
The pavement never smiled in your face and cursed you behind closed doors.

Modesto raised me more than any foster parent ever did.
The streets had their own heartbeat loud, dangerous, and real.
I learned every sound.

how the air changed before a fight,
how the streetlights hummed before they went out,
when to move, when to stay still.

7th and 9th. Crockett Street.
Those blocks knew my name.
I prayed there. Starved there. Cried there. And somehow survived there.

The same alley that took everything from me also gave me a kind of strength I didn't know existed.
They say the hood is struggle, but to me it was truth.
It was the only place that didn't pretend to be anything it wasn't.

THE BRAIN LEARNS THE PATTERN

The truth is, I wasn't afraid of being hurt.
I was afraid of being trapped.
That's the psychological core of complex trauma control feels like captivity.

Every time someone told me "you're safe now," my brain disagreed.
It remembered every time safety came with conditions.
"BE QUIET."
"BE GOOD."
"DON'T TELL."

By the time I hit the streets, my nervous system had turned survival into instinct.
Adrenaline became my bedtime story.
Hyper-vigilance replaced faith.
I could tell danger was coming by the way the temperature in a room changed.
I didn't need a reason to run my body was the reason.

Psychologically, I had developed avoidant trauma attachment when the mind associates love with harm and protection with pain.
So I did the only thing that made sense.
I stayed in motion.

THE GENIUS INSIDE THE WOUND

Even though I had communication problems, anger that came too fast, and the kind of trust issues that made me seem impossible beneath all that chaos was something else.
A mind that never stopped studying.
Even in pain, I was observing, analyzing, connecting patterns other people couldn't see.

Psychologists might call it hyper-intellectualization the brain's way of surviving unbearable emotion by turning pain into data.
I call it evolution.

What looked like defiance was really cognition running on overdrive.
While other kids memorized homework, I memorized human behavior.
I could read tone, tension, silence the micro-movements people didn't even know they made before they hurt you.
That kind of intelligence doesn't grow from comfort it grows from necessity.

Yes, I acted out.
Yes, I spoke in anger, mistrust, and defense.
But every explosion came from a mind burning too bright for its own cage.
A genius in the making one forged in deprivation.
Because sometimes, brilliance is the scar left behind when survival and perception collide.

These thoughts came with a price.
Every insight cost me peace.
Every awareness carved itself into my nerves.
That's the thing about a mind like mine it doesn't rest.
It remembers everything it had to learn to stay alive.

THE GENIUS MISUNDERSTOOD

The world mistook that mind for madness.
Society called me slow, defiant, difficult because genius without guidance looks like rebellion.
They couldn't see that my silence wasn't stupidity it was suppression.
I had spent my entire life learning how not to speak, how to hide what was happening inside my head so I wouldn't be punished for it.

I wasn't broken. I was untranslated.
A gifted mind raised in a house that feared intelligence learns to bury its own brilliance.
I just didn't know how to let it out.

It took years of self-reflection, counseling, and clawing my way back through everything I'd been taught to fear before I finally understood.
I wasn't missing anything.
I already had me all along.

THE STREETS DON'T LIE

The streets became my teacher cold, unforgiving, but real.
They taught me to read silence like a language.
They taught me that nobody is coming to save you, but you can still save yourself.
They didn't feed my body, but they fed my spirit.

Maybe that's why, no matter how far I go, I still carry those streets inside me.
Because that's where I learned the truest law of survival.
When the world throws you away, you don't disappear.
You adapt.
You shed your fear like dead skin.
You keep walking.

Psychologically, that's the cruelest truth about survival it's not healing, it's functioning.
It's the art of staying alive in environments that were never designed to let you live.

I didn't need their houses or their fake comfort.
The system starved me.
The streets showed me how to eat.

They didn't save me.
They made me remember what saving myself felt like.

Chapter 9
— The One I Loved Most
(My First Yes)

Suddenly there he was glowing.
A light I could feel before I could name it comfort, safety, love that felt like it had been waiting for me.
He was the one who would make me and break me in the same breath the one who could bring me to my knees, the one who could make me try again.
The one I loved most.

When two souls collide like mirrors, everything slows. The air changes. The noise of the world disappears until it's only heartbeat against heartbeat.
That's what it was like the first time a yes so deep it rewrote what love even meant to me.

THE COLLISION

Life didn't make it easy.
We were torn apart more than once by distance, by people who wanted to see us fail but somehow, we always found our way back.

Even when others whispered lies, we ran toward each other.
We ran all the way to San Francisco two kids with nothing but faith.
We slept in a car, split food, built a life out of hope and laughter.
The world saw runaways.
We saw freedom.

Then the past followed us.

THE PREDATOR BEHIND THE SMILE

He told me about the woman thirty-six when he was at the end of his sixteenth year, almost seventeen.
She called herself comfort, but she was construction a system of control wearing perfume.

At first she gave him attention, small gifts, validation that smelled like safety.
To a boy starved for nurture, her praise was oxygen.
She wrapped him in maternal language and romantic touch until the two became indistinguishable.
That's how grooming works it dismantles boundaries one cell at a time until captivity feels like choice.

Psychologically, it's called trauma-bond conditioning reward, withdraw, reward again.
It rewires the brain's dopamine system so pain becomes proof of devotion.
Every apology deepens dependence every crisis becomes intimacy.
By the time he realized something was wrong, the chemical leash was already fastened.

She made herself irreplaceable.
She fed him just enough affection to keep him starving.
She called him man before he'd even finished being a boy, then punished him for not being strong enough to carry her loneliness.

She stole his adolescence and replaced it with servitude disguised as love.
And when her control started to slip, she tightened the bond through pregnancy biological shackles forged from guilt.
That's not parenting. That's possession.
Even now, years later, they tell themselves it's love.
But psychology says otherwise.

What they call devotion is the residue of control a nervous system still obeying the person who trained it to confuse pain with purpose.

He defends her not because she deserves defense, but because his survival depends on believing the abuse was affection.
If he admitted she violated him, he'd have to rebuild his entire identity from the ruins she created.
So instead, he protects the cage.

That's what long-term grooming does it doesn't just steal your youth it colonizes your mind.
You begin to mistake obedience for loyalty, exhaustion for devotion.
You start to think the prison is a partnership.

THE CRASH

Even knowing all that, our love felt unbreakable until the crash.
Metal screamed, glass shattered, and the next thing I knew I was under bright lights while a doctor spoke words that changed everything pregnant.

He warned that the trauma might take the baby.
When I told the one I loved, his face lit up.
He placed his hand on my stomach and whispered how happy he was.For the first time in my life I believed maybe everything broken in me could heal.

But life turns fast.
Weeks later the bleeding began.
The first hospital said the baby was fine, but it didn't stop.
It grew worse until I ended up back under those same lights.
He drove me there but stayed outside. His family told him not to go in.
Inside, I faced it alone.with a mom mentally gone.Ten hours later my body let go.

Silence filled the room the kind that hums louder than sound.
I turned to my mother and told her to leave not from hate, but because I couldn't hold her pain and mine at once.
I walked out empty physically, spiritually, completely.

AFTER THE LOSS

When I went back to him, he wasn't the same.
Maybe the loss broke him too.
Maybe he couldn't stand to look at what we'd lost.
Maybe he chose to stand beside the baby he could hold instead of the one he couldn't.

I'll never know.
What I do know is that the warmth was gone.
I was left alone in that house days without food, without words treated like grief was a crime.

He once told me:
"Maybe this happened for a reason. Maybe you didn't deserve that baby."

How could someone who once looked at me with such light say that?
Maybe because she was still whispering through him.
When a manipulator builds your reality, her voice becomes the one you think in.

THE CONTINUING CONTROL

The older woman never stopped.
A year later, I was pregnant again, I saw her outside the library.
She hurled cups at me, screaming lies meant to shred dignity.
Later she attacked from behind screens Facebook messages claiming I'd confessed to an affair.
The logic didn't matter power did.
If she could make me react, she still owned the narrative.

When she accused me, he panicked and what came next wasn't silence. It was cruelty.

He sent a chain of messages to prove his loyalty to her.
Each one sharpened for her approval, each one a small betrayal cut into text.
He called me names that tasted like rust and ash, words he never would've formed on his own.
They were her vocabulary, written in his voice.

That's the psychology of coercive control humiliation disguised as proof.
Abusers don't just demand obedience they demand performance.
And he performed, every cruel word another offering to keep his access to the child she held hostage.

He told me I would never be half the woman she was.
I stared at the screen, my heart steady, my mind clear.

My love, you're right, I thought.
I could never be the woman she is because when you and I were together, I was still a child.

And the mother in me wanted to whisper back,
but you were too, my sweet love.

THE PATTERN

If only he could see it now the invisible leash still wrapped around his throat.
He mistakes dependence for destiny because his brain was trained that way.
Neuroscience calls it learned attachment distortion when the body bonds to its abuser as a survival mechanism.
It's not loyalty it's conditioning.
She rewards his obedience, withdraws affection when he resists, then rewards again a cycle so old it feels like home.
That's not partnership.
That's programming.

And even if they both believe it's love, it isn't.
It's trauma rehearsing its lines.
A relationship built on control can imitate devotion but never sustain freedom.

THE MIRROR

I used to wonder why I chose someone like him.
Now I see it I was replaying the script I was born into.
My mother's first love poisoned her veins and betrayed her with her own sister.

When you grow up inside that kind of distortion, chaos becomes comfort.
You call instability passion.
You mistake adrenaline for connection.

I thought I could rewrite her story, prove that love could heal what destroyed her.
But trauma repeats until it's faced.

We were trauma twins two wounded kids trying to build safety out of each other's cracks.
I thought he was my first yes because of love.
Really, he was my first yes because I was still trying to save my mother through him.

THE AFTERMATH

He couldn't face what we lost, so he turned away.
I learned to live with it.

I'll never forget the baby I lost.
I'll never forget the boy who said yes with me.
And I'll never forget that even in the deepest pain, I kept my promise to survive. The light in my living children proves every cruel word wrong.
Their laughter, their eyes, their lives are my answer.

was never undeserving. I was chosen to carry love even when one of those loves never made it into this world.

He told me one day I'd regret losing him because I couldn't be everything he needed me to be.
He wanted me to be more like a woman, which was insane because we were both kids.
And there may be a story behind his eyes that I'll never know no child grows up too soon for no reason.

But I remember what I said back.
I told him, "Well, one day you're gonna regret this because I'm gonna be famous."
He laughed and said, "Come on, be for real."

Maybe he thought it was a joke.
But here we are.
And I guess this book is me keeping my word.

Chapter 10
— The Ones Who Broke the Meaning of Love

After the one I loved most left me, I ended up back in the system. Another file. Another placement. Another promise of safety that never felt real.

I used to think love was supposed to save you.
Now I know love can destroy you too and sometimes that destruction is the doorway to finding yourself.

The ones who broke the meaning of love were the ones I trusted the most family, lovers, people who swore they'd never hurt me. They didn't just wound me; they taught me how affection can hide control and how silence can become a weapon.

THE SYSTEM REPEATS THE PATTERN

When I was seventeen, living in a foster home, another adult entered my life.
He was thirty grown, confident, already close with the foster mother who was supposed to protect me.

She drank most nights and barely kept food in the house.
Hunger does something to you.
It makes attention feel like love and kindness feel like safety.

He offered small comforts rides, meals, soft words that sounded like care but every gesture carried an unspoken debt.
I see it now he was studying my emptiness and feeding it just enough to keep me obedient.
What he called affection was control dressed up as protection.
By the time I learned he was exploiting women, I was already pregnant.That pregnancy gave me my first living child and a lifetime of mixed emotions.

I believe he wanted it that way, believing a baby would keep me tied to him.
But motherhood became my escape.
When I realized what he really was, I left and never looked back.

Later he went to prison, and I was left to face the truth of what had happened
I hadn't chosen him.
I had been conditioned by years of neglect to mistake control for care.

THE PSYCHOLOGY OF REPETITION

What happened to me wasn't coincidence it was psychological patterning.

When a child grows up in an environment where love and fear coexist, the brain fuses them together.
Safety becomes confusion.
Affection becomes anxiety.
You start to crave the very thing that hurts you because pain is the only kind of love you've ever been shown.

That's how trauma rewires attachment.
Psychologists call it trauma reenactment the unconscious drive to repeat old pain in new relationships, hoping to change the ending this time.
But until the wound is healed, every "new beginning" is just the same story wearing a different face.

I repeated the same cycle as the one I loved most, just as he had repeated his.
He was taken by a woman twice his age who disguised power as devotion.
I was taken by a man who did the same.

Two wounded souls walking separate roads that led to the same place the illusion of love built on control.

THE INHERITANCE OF VULNERABILITY

It mirrored my mother's story almost perfectly.
She had a history of being in relationships like that men who saw her light and mistook it for something they could own.

Her first love poisoned her veins and betrayed her with her own sister.
She spent the rest of her life trying to rebuild trust with people who only knew how to take.

That's just what he was doing to me using my hunger and my trust.
Two generations of women taken in by men who saw vulnerability as opportunity.
Different faces. Same pattern.
Love twisted into power.

Psychologically, it's called intergenerational trauma transmission the silent inheritance passed down not through blood, but through behavior.
When a child watches her mother tolerate pain and call it love, she learns to normalize that pain as the cost of affection.
She doesn't repeat the trauma because she wants to she repeats it because her body confuses familiarity with safety.

I didn't realize it then, but I was living the echo of my mother's heartbreak.
We were both trying to turn pain into purpose.

Both trying to be loved enough to feel safe.
Both finding predators who recognized that need before we did.

"I wasn't just trying to save my mother through them I was trying to prove that love could still reach the ones who hurt, the ones who needed saving most. And I carried that mission into every relationship that followed, believing that if I could just love deeply enough, I could undo what broke her."

THE ANATOMY OF MANIPULATION

That's how manipulation works.
It starts with pampering with promises that feel like safety.
Then come the rules, the guilt, the dependence.

It feels like love because it's all you've ever been shown.
But it isn't love.
It's ownership disguised as devotion.

Abusers don't look for weakness.
They look for strength that's been starved.
They sense the fight still flickering inside you and convince you it's love when you burn it for them.

That's what he did to me.
What she did to him.
What countless people did to my mother.

Each of us caught in the same psychological loop.
trying to prove our worth to people who only valued control.

THE BREAK IN THE CYCLE

Motherhood saved me.
It forced me to choose life over loyalty to pain.
Carrying my child was the moment the cycle cracked I refused to let another generation inherit that silence.

It's strange how life circles back.
Writing about the one I called My First Yes made me see this story more clearly.

Both men were older.
Both used power as affection.
Both left me with something to raise one a child, one a memory.

I believe God lets us walk through certain fires to understand others.
Seeing the pattern helped me forgive not because they deserved it, but because I needed the weight gone.

Understanding what was done to me helped me understand him too the boy who never escaped his own manipulation.
A victim doesn't know they're a victim when they're still surviving the abuse.

When I finally saw that, the anger softened.
I could grieve what happened to both of us and start to find peace with my loss, with his silence, with my own reflection.

REDEFINING LOVE

Love, I learned, was never meant to be ownership.
It was meant to be presence.
And sometimes you have to lose everyone who misused the word love to finally understand what it means.

Because love that controls isn't love it's fear wearing a mask. And I don't wear masks anymore.

Chapter 11
— My Brother's Shadow

Before the world began dividing us, it was just the three of us my mother, my brother, and me suspended in a brief, sacred calm that I didn't yet know was temporary.
We were the two closest in age, bound in ways we couldn't explain.
Two tiny souls orbiting each other, finding comfort in the smallness of our world.
He was laughter.
I was light.
And she was the fragile gravity holding us both together.

That time was short, but it became the place my body still returns to the only proof I ever had that peace was real.

When they came for him, something inside me cracked.
The court called it custody.
The adults called it structure.
But to me, it felt like someone reached into our chest and took half a heartbeat.
He went with his father. I stayed.
Cherry let him go not because she wanted to lose him, but because she knew what would happen if she didn't.
She knew what I would one day face the control, the starvation, the silence.
She couldn't save us both, so she did what trauma teaches mothers to do she saved what she could, however she could.
She broke the cycle in one direction and left me inside it with a purpose.

I had four brothers.
The oldest was taken early, claimed by the Monarch's need for power.
The three who came after him all shared the same father the one

she trusted to keep them safe.
Later came my sister, and she released her too.

Every separation was a wound she chose to carry so her children wouldn't have to.
But me I was the one she couldn't free.
My father lived in the grip of schizophrenia, trapped inside a mind that couldn't protect even itself.
There was no one to hand me to, no safety waiting beyond that door.
So she kept me, not because I was safer but because I was the one she believed could endure.

That's what trauma does it divides a mother's love into survival and sacrifice.
She gave my siblings distance and she gave me endurance.
They were her escape.
I was her fire.

And that's what I mean when I say I was her light.
It wasn't innocence she was protecting it was her truth.
Every part of her that the world tried to erase lived on in me.
When people silenced her, I became her voice.
When they called her broken, I became her proof that she had once glowed.
She carried the match until her hands bled, then placed it in mine so something of her would keep burning.
I was what she couldn't be anymore the living continuation of her fight to exist in a world that told her she was too much.
And she knew, even if it killed her, that I would carry that light through every dark room her silence once filled.

When my brother and I found each other again years later, it was like seeing the shadow of a star I hadn't realized had gone out.
He looked older, quieter shaped by distance.
I was louder, sharper shaped by survival.
He learned that love leaves.
I learned that love hurts.
But both of us were still lit by the same source her.

He carried her mercy.
I carried her fire.

If my brother ever reads this, I want him to know
She didn't walk away because she didn't love you.
She walked away because she couldn't love you and keep you safe in the same breath.
You were the proof that she could save something from the storm.
I was the proof that she could still love someone inside it.

She gave you distance to protect your peace.
She gave me endurance to protect her truth.
You were her calm.
I was her continuation.
She passed you off to break the cycle in one direction, and she left me behind to keep the light alive.

Two tiny souls orbiting each other one carried into freedom, the other into fire.
But the fire didn't destroy me.
It turned into something holy.
And every time I write her name, I feel that same warmth from the beginning the glow she gave me when the world still believed we were too small to matter.

That's what her light was.
It wasn't meant to shine quietly it was meant to survive.
And through me, it still does.
That was her Inheritance of Wings.

MY FATHER'S REFLECTION

My father was no stranger to crossing boundaries. He had learned the same broken version of love that shaped everyone before him.
When he showed up years later, it was near Christmas the kind of day that pretends at healing. I wanted to believe he had changed.

I wanted to believe I could have a father who wasn't a ghost of pain wearing a smile.

He arrived with gifts, a soft voice, and eyes that flickered with the kind of charm people mistake for warmth. For a moment, I believed in that illusion. But illusion doesn't survive contact with truth. In one instant, the mask slipped, and the air between us shifted the familiar chill of violation crept back in.

In that moment, I felt every cell in my body remember powerlessness. But I wasn't that child anymore. I turned toward him, looked him in the eyes, and said the words that generations of silence had swallowed before me-Leave.
And he did.

That moment lasted only seconds, but it took a lifetime of pain to reach it. It was the first time in my bloodline someone chose self-protection over silence. It was the moment I broke a thousand unspoken rules the ones that teach daughters to keep the peace, even when it destroys them. Psychologically, that was the turning point where trauma stopped dictating the script and autonomy rewrote it.

MY MOTHER'S MIRROR

So much of this confusion began with my mother. From the moment she could see her reflection, she was told her beauty was her only worth. People treated her face like property something to own, envy, or punish.
When the world convinced her that beauty was survival, she learned to weaponize it.

That's the cruelty of psychological conditioning when a woman's value is built on how she looks, she spends her life chasing validation that always runs faster than she can. My mother's mirror was both her armor and her wound. She learned to control what others saw because no one ever cared to see her.

I can still picture her sitting in front of that small mirror, the smell of cheap vanilla perfume and old Cover Girl powder heavy in the air. She wasn't getting ready to go anywhere; she was getting ready to survive. Each stroke of makeup was a prayer for control in a world that had taken hers away. She painted her face not out of vanity but out of self-defense.

That's what trauma does it teaches you to disguise your pain as presentation.

THE INHERITANCE OF CONFUSION

In families where trauma stays unspoken, love becomes distorted.
Children raised in secrecy crave the people who hurt them, because the brain confuses familiarity with safety. It's called trauma bonding the emotional loop where affection and fear blur together until you can't tell them apart.

My mother was taught that attention equals worth.
My father was taught that control equals power.
And my brother learned both.

Each of them carried forward a version of the same confusion the belief that love must wound you before it can prove itself real. And me? I carried the awareness of it all the pattern, the silence, the ache and finally, the language to name it.

That's the cruel blessing of being the one who sees clearly you inherit the map, but you also inherit the weight of knowing where every scar came from.

BREAKING THE PATTERN

In my family, silence was the inheritance.
Each generation repeated the same story, only the faces changed.
Children learned to protect the secrets that destroyed them, mistaking loyalty for love.

That's called trans-generational trauma the repetition of pain disguised as duty. The only way to stop it is to speak the truth out loud and refuse to play the part.

So I did.
I became the one who said enough.

When I think of my brother now, I don't feel hate.
I feel grief for the boy he was, for the man he became, for the childhood that neither of us got to keep.
I see my parents, too two people who were both victims of the same inheritance, taught that love must break you before it can save you.

But I'm here to write a different ending.
Because I finally know what none of them were ever allowed to learn.

Real love doesn't demand your silence. Real love never asks you to disappear to be worthy of it.

THE BROTHER I NEEDED MOST

Although a different Brother, The same baby the Monarch once took from my mother grew into the one who would hurt me the most the one who would beat me, torment me, and was even encouraged to do so. I endured violence at his hands for years. I don't know how he couldn't love me. I don't know how he couldn't see how much I needed him.

It was a deeper betrayal than the Monarch's. Her cruelty I expected it was the language of control I'd known my whole life. But his? His felt sacred. Because I needed him more than I ever needed her. There's a spiritual kind of bond between siblings that you can't put into words, and that's what made it cut so deep.

Maybe he couldn't accept what I represented. Maybe I was the truth he couldn't bear the living proof that the Monarch was never really his mother, that everything he believed about his place in this family was built on lies. I don't know.

But I never blamed him. Not for one punch. Not for one cruel word. My love for him never could even if he doesn't love me. That's the same light I was talking about with my mother continuing to think love can save. that's what trauma does it makes you protect the one who hurt you most, because losing them would mean losing the hope that love could ever save what broke you.

THE TWIN I NEVER HAD TO NAME

There was another one just as close to me as my own brother. We were born only eleven days apart, two souls in the same month fighting the same silent war. Different mothers. Different homes. Different ways of seeing the world. But somehow, we were mirrors. I was his reflection, and maybe even the reflection of his mother too. I know it hurt him seeing me was like seeing everything he couldn't fix.

He was all I had. The only one who ever truly seemed to understand the language of my silence. But even he couldn't escape the system. It reached for him too, reshaping his memories, rewriting the truth in his own mind until he could almost believe it wasn't as bad as it was. Over time, I watched the warmth fade. The light that once saw me whole grew colder, more distant.

Yet I know he remembers. I know it still burns inside him, even when he tries to forget. He feels me on a spiritual level I am the one piece of his bloodline he can never erase. And still, he pretends not to know me. He stands quiet in the face of everything we both saw, everything he knows they did to me, and to his mother too. But that silence isn't indifference it's the weight of survival. It's the fear of facing the truth that could undo him.

I confronted that truth, and it broke him open. He couldn't take it. Still, I can't hate him for that. Because I know the boy he was. I know the man he became. I know he's trying to make sense of it all the only way he knows how. Nobody ever told him that there's another way that he can speak, that he can tell the truth, and that it will be okay. Nobody told him that he could stop the cycle.

And even now, after everything, I love him. Because in that brief mirror of our youth, God placed him there to show me that someone did see me, even if he couldn't save me. He was my twin in spirit, and no lie or silence can change that.

I have another brother that I don't believe has ever said two words to me my entire life.
And then there's another brother this one wasn't untouched by the system either. We were all marked in different ways, even if some of us tried to pretend otherwise.
I passed the silence, but maybe my sister won't have to carry the psychology of it. Maybe she'll get to live without the weight of what we inherited.

Then a baby came.
He wasn't my brother he was my baby.
We spent every single day together.

It's kind of ironic, because the day he came home, they told me I wasn't allowed to touch him.
That just proves how powerful my presence was how even my love could interfere with their control.

But I know he knows.
I know he can feel that I took care of him that my love for him was motherly, even though I was just a baby myself.

But even he changed.
He wasn't untouched by the system either.
He forgot how he used to cry for me to hold him.
I changed him. I fed him.
I held him while he cried for his mom when she left
and I felt every tear like it was my own.

He must believe that I'm not worthy enough,
So he tells himself I didn't have it that bad.
He has to pretend he didn't see it.

He didn't know why I had to leave.
Even he was manipulated into hating me.

But I can't blame him.
I can't help but love him.
It's that voice inside my soul my mother's arms reaching out
whispering, love can save him.
And even though I know the system, even though I understand
the psychology, even though I know love can't save him…
I'm going to give it anyway. Even if it's not possible for him to ever
love me back I'm used to it. I can deal with it.

Chapter 12
— I Won't Be Garbage

After a failed marriage one that ended in betrayal I found myself right back at the bottom.
My husband cheated on me, and when the truth came out, it left me standing in the middle of everything I thought I'd built, just collapsing around me.
No partner. No help.
Just me, my daughter, and my three beautiful boys.

I was in an after-care program from foster care what they called support but it never felt like support.
It felt like surveillance.
Like someone was always watching, waiting for me to mess up. Another system keeping tabs, another set of eyes searching for proof that I'd become exactly what they expected me to be.

Time went on, and the marriage that broke me left me with three more miracles my boys and barely enough to survive on.
I was living off almost nothing every month, sitting in low-income housing, the heater barely working, my kids all asleep under a pile of blankets.

I remember sitting there one night quiet, the kind of quiet that hums in your bones and I looked around and thought: This is what they expected of me.

A single mom on welfare.
Another case file.
Another product of the system.

But deep down, I knew I wasn't that.
I WASN'T GARBAGE.
I WASN'T BROKEN.
I wasn't going to let their idea of me become my truth.

That night something switched in me.
It wasn't rage. It was realization.
I told myself, I won't be garbage.
And that became my fire.

THE RISE

It started with nursing school.
I didn't know what I was doing, but I knew I was doing something.
I worked, studied, raised my kids, and made it happen.

Then I went further Paramedic Academy.
I pushed myself harder.
And I graduated.

Every step I took was a message not just to the world, but to myself that I could do what nobody expected me to do.

But underneath that drive was the psychology of someone who was never supposed to succeed.
When you grow up being told you're worthless, success feels foreign.
You question every good thing that happens.
You prepare for collapse.
You think small because no one ever showed you what thriving looks like.

That's what happens when people label you before they even know you you start to live like the label fits.

But the truth is, I always had it in me.
Art ran through my veins drawing, poetry, hair, cake sculpting, photo editing, makeup.
Creativity was my rebellion.
And that's what scared them.

THE PSYCHOLOGY OF SUPPRESSION

That's what suppression looks like.
When people sense your power before you do, they'll do anything to keep you small.

They'll lie to you.
They'll make you doubt your gifts.
They'll convince you your light is arrogance and your confidence is danger.

The psychology behind it is simple
They weren't protecting me.
They were protecting their comfort.

They knew that if I ever stepped fully into my own light, I'd outgrow the cage they built for me.
And I did.

Because what I went through wasn't much different from what my mother went through.
Her story and mine run parallel two women made of fire, punished for burning too bright.

She gave her love to people who couldn't handle her light.
People who mistook her softness for surrender and her beauty for something they could own.
She was betrayed, abandoned, and judged by people who never saw the woman she was underneath the pain.

THE BLACK-OUT LONELINESS

And then there were those months the ones that changed me forever.

I spent months alone in that cold apartment with my kids, living off food stamps, counting every can in the cupboard.
No calls. No visitors.
Just silence thick enough to hear my thoughts pacing the room.

Days blurred into weeks, and weeks into months until time lost shape.
Morning looked like night; night looked like another morning.
Even the walls began to hum with the weight of waiting.

That's when it hit me this was her silence.
The black-out loneliness my mother must have lived in.
That place where you cut everyone you love because peace costs isolation, and the quiet starts to sound like ghosts.

In that stillness, something inside me cracked open.
Peace isn't peaceful when you've lived your whole life in chaos.
At first, it's unbearable.
Because when the world finally stops screaming, you start hearing the parts of yourself that were buried under the noise.

That's where the real demons live not outside, but in the echo.
The mind starts replaying every betrayal, every hunger, every face that said you'll never make it.
And you realize the loudest voice tearing you apart isn't theirs anymore.
It's yours.

That's the psychology of survival fatigue when your brain no longer knows how to rest without panicking.
When safety feels like suffocation because your body's been trained to equate calm with danger.
I was living inside that paradox desperate for peace but terrified of it.
But it was in that months-long black-hole silence that I finally met myself.
Not the version they defined, not the case number, not the survivor.

The woman.
The artist.
The mother.
The fighter who refuses to die in anyone else's story.

THE BREAK IN THE BLOODLINE

I think now that I was meant to relive her story not to repeat it, but to finish it.
She didn't have the tools, the education, or the support to rewrite her ending.
But I do.

I carry her blood, but I also carry her unfinished story.
And I'm turning it into strength.

Now I live differently.
I keep learning.
I keep growing.
I keep proving that I am more than every whisper, every statistic, every box they tried to bury me in.

Because I didn't just make it.
I became more.

THE INHERITANCE OF FIRE

I won't be garbage.
I never was.
And neither was she.

We were just two women the world underestimated two flames that refused to go out.

She handed me the silence that haunted her, and I turned it into language.
She handed me her loneliness, and I built a life from it.
She handed me her brokenness, and I made art.

I was born to finish the story she couldn't.
And I did.

Chapter 13
— Something to Live For

When I lost my baby, I lost myself too.
When the one I loved most walked away, everything inside me just stopped.
I stopped eating, stopped sleeping, stopped trying.

I was ninety pounds of heartbreak, exhaustion, and silence.
I laid there for months numb, empty, disappearing piece by piece.
The streets became my bed.
I didn't care if I made it to the next day.
I was homeless, starving, and holding on by a thread, waiting for something anything that could make the pain stop.

I used to tell myself maybe he'd come back.
Maybe he'd see how bad I was falling apart and finally come home.
God knows I needed him at that time, and maybe God knows exactly why He didn't let that happen.

Eventually, it landed me right back in foster care at seventeen years old.
I didn't want to go back.
I wanted to prove I could survive on my own, but survival has a way of forcing you back into the very places you swore you'd never return to.
I had no one, nothing, and nowhere to go.
I was just done.

There were nights I lay awake thinking how easy it would be to just disappear, and the only thing that stopped me was that faint voice of God whispering, It's a sin. Don't do it. Hold on.

That was the only thing keeping me alive God's voice and a fragile thread of hope that somehow, my story wasn't over.

AND THEN SHE CAME

So beautiful.
So pure.
Heaven-sent.

Ivory skin, dark hair, eyes that started deep blue but slowly turned green just like I somehow knew they would.
My redemption wrapped in a tiny blanket.
My proof that God never left me, even when I thought He did.

I held her in my arms, and everything changed.

I swallowed her. I loved her. I melted into her.
She was my beauty, my love, my hope, my gift, my salvation everything I was, walking outside of my body.
My very heart with its own heartbeat.

I remember staring at her little face thinking, Oh my God… this is love.
Real. Raw. Steady. The kind that doesn't go anywhere. The kind that stays.

A mother can't just leave this.

WHEN THE MIND MEETS THE MOMENT

Something clicks when you hold your baby for the first time.
It isn't just emotion it's biology.
The brain floods with oxytocin, dopamine, and serotonin all at once, rewiring every instinct you've ever had.
It's the body's way of saying, You belong to each other now.

Psychologically, that moment births more than a child it births identity.
Every wound, every scar, every loss rearranges itself around this new life.
Grief makes room for purpose.
You stop asking Why am I here? and start whispering For you. For this.

In trauma psychology, they call it post-traumatic growth when devastation becomes the soil for transformation.
It doesn't erase the pain; it gives it direction.
That's what motherhood did to me. It didn't heal me it gave my pain somewhere to live that wasn't inside my chest.

SEEING MY MOTHER IN THE MIRROR

That's when everything started falling into place.
That's when I started seeing my mother in the mirror.

Because I finally understood what broken really looks like not the kind people point at and judge, but the kind that comes from being stripped of everything you love; from having your child taken before you ever even get to hold them; from being forced into silence while the world blames you for your own pain.

That's what my mother went through when The Monarch took control of her first baby.

She didn't leave because she didn't love.
She left because she was destroyed.

Sitting there holding my baby, I thought, How broken does someone have to be to walk away from this?

And that's when I knew my mother didn't walk away.
She was pushed.
She was cornered.
She was hurting in ways I had never understood before.

The psychology behind it made everything make sense the chaos, the addiction, the distance.
They were symptoms of grief.
They were her way of coping with the kind of pain that rearranges your soul.

And in that moment, I stopped being angry.
I stopped blaming her.
Because I finally saw the woman behind the mistakes the woman who loved her children but never got to heal from her own loss.

When I held my baby, I felt what she must've felt the love, the fear, the desperation to protect.
And I realized that maybe I had to go through my own heartbreak just to understand hers.

CHOOSING PAIN TO PROTECT LOVE

When the doctors told me I could deliver naturally, I said no.
I told them to cut me open.

I needed to see her safe.
I needed to know she was breathing.
I needed to know God was keeping His promise.

I chose the pain because after losing one child, I wasn't willing to risk another.
That's maternal psychology in its rawest form a mind that would rather endure agony than uncertainty.
Fear becomes instinct.
Pain becomes prayer.

REBIRTH

She taught me the greatest lesson of all that I wasn't meant to die, that I wasn't garbage, that I wasn't a mistake.

Before her, I had nothing to live for.
After her, I had everything.

She didn't just save me.
She rebuilt me.
She gave me back my will, my strength, my meaning.

The one I loved most may have brought me to my knees,
but my daughter made me rise higher than I ever thought I could.

And somewhere in that rise,
I forgave my mother.

Because I finally understood she didn't fail me.
The world failed her.

Chapter 14
— The Ghosts That Stay

The ghosts that stay aren't the kind that knock on walls or whisper in the dark.
They don't haunt houses. They haunt bodies.
They live behind your eyes, in the hollow of your throat, in the way you flinch at a footstep.

People think ghosts are about death. They're not.
They're about what doesn't die the pain, the memory, the handed-down ache that keeps replaying itself until you start to think it's the only real thing.

My family's treatment toward me made me feel like I was walking inside someone else's wound.
I could never shake her shadow.
Every time I caught my reflection, I saw my mother's outline staring back not only her face but the exhaustion in her jaw, the way her hope ended before it could start.
She numbed.
I didn't.
That was the only difference I could name, and even that felt fragile.

They tell you the brain heals, but the brain also remembers.
When trauma loops, it trains the nervous system to expect betrayal, to prefer what it knows even when what it knows kills it slowly.
Psychologists call it intergenerational transmission not a curse, but a pattern: love and loss folded into the wiring of a child's brain until they become indistinguishable.

I learned to read that wiring in myself the way my body tensed at a closing door, how I waited for an absence to become abuse, how my stomach catalogued every look that might turn into harm.

Every time life cut me open, I reached for something therapy, prayer, education, anything to climb out.
She reached for silence.
For escape.
For numbness.
And I can't blame her.

I've stared at a bottle of pills too, thinking how simple it would be to end the noise.
And then it hit me this is what she faced.

That realization didn't free me.
It filled me.
It rewired my anger into understanding.
Every scar on my body, every wound that healed wrong that's where she lives.
Not as a ghost that haunts me, but as a story I'm still trying to understand.

It's painful realizing we were built from the same roots.
Haunting to know the things that broke her are the same things I've had to fight my way through.
The same chemicals that shaped her suffering shaped my resilience.
The same silence that buried her became my search for truth.

THE FUNERAL

And then came the day of her funeral.

When my mother died, I was twenty-eight old enough to have lived her story, young enough to still believe I could change the ending.
There's something cruel about losing a parent at the exact age you finally understand them.

The psychology of it is brutal the attachment figure whose wounds sculpted your own disappears, and the brain scrambles for closure that can never come.
Grief at that age isn't childish it's clinical.
You don't cry like a daughter you unravel like a mirror that suddenly realizes who it's been reflecting all along.
Her death froze me between comprehension and forgiveness twenty-eight years of echoes, then silence.

The year didn't just hit me because of her death it hit because I was the same age she'd been when her spirit first started leaving her body.
It was like our timelines folded over each other.
I began to feel things I knew she once felt the exhaustion that lives behind the ribs, the quiet panic that masquerades as calm.
It was as if her unfinished emotions had been waiting for me to reach that exact age so they could crawl back through my skin.
That realization haunted me.
I started understanding things I knew she must have understood long before I did, and the knowing itself became a kind of inheritance one that burned instead of blessed.

It was just me and my brother standing there alone.
No flowers.
No crowd.
No noise.
Just silence, and the weight of everything she never received in this life.

All she ever wanted was love.
Affection.
Acceptance.
Even in death, she didn't get acknowledgment not from the people who should've been there, not from the ones who claimed they cared.

That moment swallowed me whole.
Because I realized the same loneliness that haunted her had been

haunting me my whole life.
That same quiet onlyness -the kind that sits heavy in your chest when you realize you have nobody.

Solo Christmases.
Empty holidays.
No grandparents for my children.
No real family.
Just memories of foster homes and the long list of people who failed me.

And the truth is, even the ones who didn't throw the punches were guilty too.
Because they stood by and watched.
They failed to protect me.
And in some ways, that silence hurts worse than the blows ever did.

THE GHOST IN THE MIRROR

Sometimes I think her ghost doesn't just live in me it breathes through the space between what we both deserved and what we never got.

She passed this face to me.
And maybe she passed the fight too.

Because when I see her now, I don't just see the woman who was broken.
I see the woman who survived long enough to give me the chance to heal differently.

The ghosts that stay aren't meant to scare us.
They're meant to remind us where we came from and who we were born to set free.

Chapter 15
— Memory and Re-Creation

Pain has memory.
It doesn't die when the body does it migrates.
It hides in silence, in habits, in the way we love or refuse to love.
It lives inside the nervous system in the cortisol that floods without warning, in the shallow breath, in the startle that comes before thought.
That's how it travels not only through blood, but through energy through what was never spoken but always felt.

My mother's pain didn't end with her.
It found a new home in me.
Not as addiction, not as silence but as obsession.
The obsession to understand.

Why she broke.
Why I bled the same way.
Why it all felt like a script written long before I was born.

For years I called it a curse.
Now I know it was a map.

THE NEUROLOGY OF INHERITANCE

Science calls it epigenetic memory the way trauma writes itself into the chemistry of our cells.
The body remembers what the mind refuses to name.
When a parent lives in chronic fear, the child's nervous system learns the same rhythm before they can even speak.
The amygdala becomes a historian the body becomes an archive. Her fear became my intuition.

Her vigilance became my instinct.
Her pain became the way my neurons fired under stress.
And every panic, every collapse, every numb silence that came later in my life it wasn't weakness.
It was repetition.
It was biology trying to finish a story psychology hadn't yet understood.

Her breakdown was the original blueprint of my nervous system.
Her healing never arrived so my body made the attempt for her.

INHERITED COORDINATES

Her pain showed me where the landmines were buried.
Her collapse showed me where the walls would give.
Her scars drew the outline of everything I needed to rebuild differently.

She wasn't weak she was my map.
Every wound she carried was a signpost.
Every piece of her strength was a direction.
I learned to trace her patterns the way a scientist studies DNA to locate the mutation, to understand where survival twisted into fear.

Psychology calls it intergenerational transmission how unresolved trauma seeks resolution in the next generation until someone is brave enough to stop running and start naming.
That someone was me.

I looked straight into what destroyed her and said, Not again.

That's what re-creation really is not pretending the pain didn't happen, but giving it new architecture so it can't destroy you again.

RECONSTRUCTION

My mother didn't have the tools to decode her own suffering.
She left me the evidence instead the symptoms, the silences, the contradictions.
Every erratic gesture was a clue. Every distance, a defense mechanism.

When I began studying trauma, everything locked into place.
The silence wasn't neglect it was avoidant attachment, the brain's way of protecting itself from more loss.
The anger wasn't cruelty it was dysregulated affect, grief with nowhere to go.
The distance wasn't rejection it was hyper-independence, a nervous system addicted to control because safety never lasted.

She didn't fail me she simply stopped where her strength ran out.
And that's exactly where mine began.

Every scar she wore was a language I had to learn.
And when I finally became fluent, I didn't echo it I rewrote it.

That's how I rebuilt her.
Through words.
Through truth.
Through creation.

Each sentence I write is her nervous system finding peace through mine.
Each paragraph is an act of neural re-patterning rewriting the story that our bodies kept repeating.

RE-CREATION

Re-creation isn't denial; it's exposure therapy for the soul.
It's taking what tried to bury you and turning it into scaffolding for something higher.

My mother didn't hand me pain as punishment.
She handed me data truth wrapped in ache.
She gave me the map, not the destination.

Her suffering became my curriculum.
Her life became my laboratory.
She was both the wound and the wisdom.

I'm stronger, not because she was weak,
but because she walked through hell first and left the path marked in ash.

That's the psychology of healing when the trauma loop finally breaks, not by forgetting, but by understanding.
When the amygdala learns to stand down.
When the body learns safety in its own skin again.

I used to think I was surviving her story.
Now I know I'm completing it.

TRANSMUTATION

Every page I write, every truth I speak, every creation I bring to life that's her love, re-formed.
That's trauma converted into testimony.
That's memory turned into movement.
That's pain becoming art.

She wasn't my burden.
She was my beginning.

And I will carry her light not her wounds into everything I create next.

Because that's how generational trauma finally ends,
not in silence,
but in language.

Chapter 16
-The Streets of Salvation

The streets taught me more than any classroom ever could.
They taught me hunger the kind that eats away at your stomach and your spirit.
They taught me fear how to sense danger before it speaks, how to move quiet, how to survive on instinct alone.

They taught me something textbooks never could that survival isn't theory it's psychology in motion.
It's the science of human behavior under threat, the study of what happens when the brain replaces safety with strategy.
The streets didn't teach through words they taught through conditioning.
They trained my nervous system before I even knew what a nervous system was.

> Every sound became data.
> Every silence became a question.
> Every breath was a decision.

That's what trauma does it doesn't disappear when the danger ends it becomes part of you.
The amygdala keeps firing, the body keeps remembering, and peace starts to feel like a lie.
I didn't just live on those streets I became them.

THE BODY KEEPS THE SCORE

That's the psychology of survival hypervigilance.
It's when your body never stops scanning, even in sleep.
It's when your heart beats faster in a quiet room than it ever did in chaos.
People think the streets harden you, but really they sensitize you; every sound, every shadow, every shift in air becomes information your body can't stop reading.

I learned to disappear before danger spoke my name.
I learned that invisibility was safety, silence was armor.
That's what psychologists call avoidant adaptation when disappearing feels safer than being seen.
It's not defiance.
It's design.

I thought the streets were punishment.
Now I know they were preparation.

HER PULSE IN MY VEINS

My mother was still alive then somewhere walking her own streets, fighting her own ghosts.
I didn't understand it at the time, but I was mirroring her nervous system, living her pain in real time.
That's intergenerational trauma the echo that passes from one body to another without words.

> **Her fear became my intuition.**
> **Her silence became my language.**
> **Her pain became my reflex.**

Psychology calls it repetition compulsion the need to unconsciously replay what hurt you in hopes of finally changing

the ending.
I didn't know it then, but every night I survived was her story continuing through me.

Even when she wasn't there, her voice lived in my bloodstream:
You've made it through worse. Keep walking.
So I did.
Every night under a bridge.
Every day without food.
Every prayer whispered into the dark.

That wasn't haunting.
That was inheritance.

That was cellular memory the body remembering the fight long after the world forgets.

THE EDUCATION OF PAIN

I didn't see it back then, but she was still teaching me through absence, through error, through pain.
She was teaching me the psychology of endurance that sometimes the only way to keep living is to let your mind leave the body for a while.
That's dissociation, the brain's last defense against unbearable reality.

Every silence from her was a syllabus.
Every mistake, a lecture.
Every scar, a degree in resilience.

She showed me that surviving isn't failure it's adaptation.
When the world collapses, the mind evolves.

That's post-traumatic adaptation not brokenness, but proof the brain will do anything to stay alive.

The streets didn't destroy me they stripped me of illusions.
They forced me to meet my rawest self the one who still believed she could make it.
That's post-traumatic growth when survival becomes insight, when pain becomes purpose.

FULL CIRCLE: THE BIRTH OF PEACE

When my daughter was born, the pattern cracked open.
The first time I looked into her eyes, I saw both of us me and my mother reflected back.
The same fire.
The same softness hiding behind the fight.
But this time, it looked like peace.

That's when I finally understood what love really is.
Not the kind that leaves you starving for proof,
but the kind that fills you after everything's been taken.
That's what psychologists call earned security when love becomes safe enough to rewire the brain's belief in safety itself.

> Through her, I saw forgiveness.
> Through her, I saw purpose.
> Through her, I saw salvation.

My mother was my salvation through pain.
My daughter became my salvation through love.
That's generational healing when the trauma stops traveling because someone finally understands it.

THE SCIENCE OF REDEMPTION

Love re-wrote the chemistry of my brain.
Oxytocin quieted the cortisol.
Safety replaced survival.
And for the first time, my body believed it was allowed to rest.

That's what recovery really is when your body finally learns that the war is over.
When you stop existing as a reflex and start living as a choice.

The streets didn't ruin me; they revealed me.
They taught me that salvation doesn't always fall from heaven.
Sometimes it rises from the same hell that tried to bury you.
Sometimes it's born crying in your arms, proof that the story didn't end it transformed.

My mother's fight became my survival.
My survival became my daughter's safety.
That's the real inheritance not pain, but proof.

The streets were my first classroom.
Motherhood was my graduation.
And love not fragile, conditional love, but the kind that rebuilds what the world tried to erase became my psychology, my redemption, my salvation.

Chapter 17
— Strawberry Wine with Cherry

My mother's name was Cherry, and even her name sounded like something soft and sweet.
She had that kind of beauty that made you stop mid-sentence long auburn hair that caught the light like fire, green eyes that glowed like wet leaves, skin so pale it almost shimmered.
Her laugh was delicate, smooth the kind that could fill a room and still sound lonely.

I see her in memory the same way every time sitting at the kitchen table, a cigarette in her hand, the smoke curling around her like a veil she never lifted.
She moved slowly, deliberately, every gesture part of some unspoken choreography a woman holding herself together one graceful breath at a time.
Even when she was unraveling, she made it look intentional.
That was her art the performance of survival.

When I was little, Strawberry Wine played on repeat.
I thought it was just her favorite song.
She'd hum it under her breath while cooking, while crying, while staring into nothing.
Her voice always drifted somewhere else when she sang, like she was standing in two timelines at once the woman I knew and the girl she used to be.

BREAKING THE CODE

I didn't sing.
I JUST LISTENED.
And years later, I finally broke the code.

She wasn't just singing a song she was singing her life out through it.
Every lyric was a breadcrumb leading back to the innocence she lost.
When she sang "like strawberry wine," she wasn't romanticizing first love she was grieving it the sweetness that had been taken from her too soon.

That's what trauma does it hides truth inside repetition.
Psychology calls it re-enactment the mind's desperate attempt to retell what it can't remember safely.
She couldn't say what happened, so she let the melody say it for her.
She encoded her trauma inside music, hoping someone maybe me would someday learn to hear it.

Her voice was her nervous system trying to speak.
That's somatic expression when the body releases what the mouth cannot.
Each note was an exhale of memory.
Each verse was a confession wrapped in melody.

When I realized that, the whole world went quiet.
Because I finally understood she wasn't performing.
She was remembering.
She was reliving the night she lost her girlhood and the years she spent trying to find it again.
That song was her story disguised as someone else's lyrics.
It was her way of saying, This happened to me too.

THE HIDDEN PSYCHOLOGY

The human brain protects us from unbearable truth by disguising it.
That's dissociation when pain gets filed away in sensory fragments: a smell, a song, a sound.
Cherry's trauma lived in melody.
Each time she sang, her body entered both past and present at once.
Her eyes would glaze, her voice would quiver that's what trauma recall looks like in real time.

She couldn't tell me what broke her because she didn't have the language for it.
So she left me the song as a message written in code.
And when I finally decoded it, I stopped blaming her.
Because once you know what someone survived, their silence stops sounding like neglect and starts sounding like pain.

WHAT SHE REALLY GAVE ME

She didn't hand me stories about princes or promises she handed me truth in disguise.
She taught me that pain has to go somewhere and if it can't go into words, it will leak into art.
That's emotional transference turning agony into something the heart can hold without collapsing.
Her song was her therapy session that no one attended.
And I was the witness she never knew she needed.

Now when I hear Strawberry Wine, I hear more than music.
I hear a mother translating trauma into beauty so it wouldn't kill her.
I hear the girl inside her crying from a distance she could never cross.
I hear everything she couldn't say, played at the exact frequency my soul was tuned to receive.

She wasn't addicted to the song she was addicted to remembering who she used to be.
And every time she sang, she stitched herself together for a few minutes longer.

THE LEGACY BENEATH THE MELODY

I don't sing anymore but I write. That's another story.
But through writing, I decoded her melody into meaning.
She left me poetry instead of protection.
And maybe that's what saved me.
Cherry taught me that healing doesn't always sound like hope.
Sometimes it sounds like a cracked voice whispering through smoke, singing the same song over and over until it hurts less.
She didn't teach me how to survive cleanly she taught me how to survive creatively.
And that is the difference between repeating pain and rewriting it.
Now I understand the real psychology of inheritance:
She didn't pass down addiction, or failure, or madness.
She passed down artistry.
She passed down the instinct to turn wounds into something worth hearing.

So this is for her
the woman who sang her pain in code and trusted that one day her daughter would understand the language.
The woman who taught me that trauma hides inside beauty, that loss can sound like a love song, and that sometimes the only way to survive is to make it sound sweet.
Cherry wasn't just my mother.
She was the song I was born to translate.
And now, through these pages, she finally gets to be heard not as a tragedy, but as a voice that refused to die quiet.

Strawberry Wine, July 1996

IT TAKES ME BACK TO 1996,
where memory lingers, still alive.
A song I don't know, yet it feels so near,
soft in the corner, only I can hear.
My mother was Cherry, her beauty defined, dark auburn hair like a river of wine.
In sunlight it shimmered, in shadow it burned, a crown of fire with each head she turned.
Her lips were red, her laughter sweet, vanilla followed her down every street.
Her skin was ivory, her spirit divine, her green eyes glowing, forever mine.
I look just like her, reflection the same, a mirror of blood, a carried flame.
And even as a child, before I knew love, her gaze told the story I was part of.
Strawberry Wine was her favorite song.
She'd move through the room, graceful and strong, long auburn hair dancing in the air,
her voice rising softly, carried everywhere.
She sang as though time could never be gone, her spirit alive as the music lived on.
I was a July baby, born in her song, under the hot July moon where I belong.
The same one Deana sang in that line, where innocence ripens like strawberry wine.
But she is gone now, passed from my sight, still I dream of her auburn hair in the light.
The chorus returns when I close my eyes her voice, her scent, her lullabies.

And though time has taken, the memory stays, strawberry wine on the edge of those days.
A mother named Cherry, eternal, divine, her love still lives forever mine.

Chapter 18
— Inheritance of Wings

When I say she is my reflection and I am hers, it isn't poetry. It's prophecy. It's the truth that made me tremble the day I watched my mother die because I wasn't only losing her, I was staring straight into what I would become if I didn't break the cycle.

She had already begun to fade long before her body followed. Addiction didn't start her ending; trauma did. The first crack appeared the year she realized I had become the family's next target. I was six. I remember the water still dripping from my hair after they dragged me from the bath beaten wet, humiliated, my mother listening, helplessly as they destroyed the little girl she had tried to keep safe. She tried to keep me twice she took me back twice They took me away,But the last time, when CPS took me, something in her broke for good.

That's when I lost her.
Not to death, but to despair.
Not to drugs, but to the slow erosion of a soul that can no longer bear what it knows.

You see, trauma doesn't just scar it mutates. It changes the brain's wiring until reality itself becomes unbearable. When people speak of schizophrenia as if it's madness, they miss the truth: sometimes it's the mind's last defense, the brain splitting itself apart to survive what the heart cannot hold. My mother's mind didn't "fail" her it fractured under the weight of a truth no one helped her carry.

She saw the pattern replaying. She saw me living the same pain she had swallowed her entire life. When she looked at me, she saw the same innocence the world punished her for, the same glow that made people envious and cruel. She knew what they would do to me, because they had already done it to her. And in that moment of recognition that devastating, mirror-sharp clarity something inside her surrendered.

That was the day her reflection shattered, and the day mine began.

When I looked at her on her deathbed, I wasn't just mourning a mother. I was mourning the version of myself that would have died the same way if I hadn't decided to stop the bleeding of generations. She was the warning written in flesh. I was the echo refusing to fade.

The tree of our bloodline is twisted. Its roots are tangled in silence and pain I generations watered by tears, not rain. My mother was the trunk, bearing the scars of every storm that came before her. I am the branch that grew away from the rot, but I still feel her pulse in my veins. Every time I try to rise toward the light, I feel the pull of her roots begging me not to forget.

And I don't I never will.

Because when I say she is my reflection and I am hers, I mean I carry her inside me like a haunting. I see her eyes when I'm tired, her hands in mine when I tremble, her pain in my silence. The mirror is never just a mirror it's a grave and a promise.

She died believing she was too broken to be saved. I live proving she was wrong.

But every night, when I close my eyes, I hear her whisper from the other side of that mirror
DON'T LET THEM DO TO YOU WHAT THEY DID TO ME.

And I answer:
I WON'T. BUT THEY'LL REMEMBER ME FOR IT.

My brothers always said I was our mother's favorite.
But the truth is, there were no favorites only survivors of the same house.
When she held me, she wasn't choosing me over them. She was reaching for herself through me.
She saw in me the same wounds that had once bled inside her, the same quiet fractures forming beneath my skin. She knew what was coming. She knew what it felt like.
That's what they never understood she wasn't nurturing a favorite child, she was trying to mother the broken girl still screaming inside her.
Every time she wrapped her arms around me, she was begging time to give her another chance to save herself.
What they saw as favoritism was really recognition the mirror of her own suffering staring back at her.
And that kind of love isn't soft. It's desperate. It's holy. It's the kind that doesn't heal; it haunts.

I saw myself in her.

Not a soft resemblance a mirror made of warning. A lifetime of pain taught me one hard law the more they tried to break us, the clearer I understood what had happened to her. Every scar on my skin was one I recognized in her. When you're born of someone who never had the chance to heal, you inherit more than their eyes or their name. You inherit their silence, their shame, the stories that keep breathing inside your bones.

My mother was punished for her beauty.
People don't like to admit that beauty in the wrong house can be lethal. Her light made them feel small. When envy festers close to home, it doesn't just burn it infects. Her own siblings couldn't celebrate her without trying to destroy her. They handed her the same poison that kept her trapped, all while pretending to care. They wanted control, not love. Because a woman who shines can't be owned, and that terrified them.

That's what I call pretty-girl punishment when your glow

becomes a threat, when your laughter is too loud for their comfort and your kindness too real for their lies. They don't want you healed they want you manageable, just broken enough to stay quiet. My mother's beauty became her prison. Her addiction, their weapon. Every time she tried to rise, they called it rebellion. Every time she fell, they called it deserved. They didn't save her; they sabotaged her.

And still, somehow, she kept her grace. People said she was weak. No she was exhausted. She had been handed everyone else's pain since childhood, and when she could no longer hold it, they named her the problem. That's what families do when they can't face the truth they make a scapegoat. Once the blame is placed, it becomes law.

She wore that role before I was even born. She was their mirror, and they hated what it showed. They saw me in her, and her in me and they hated it. When I grew old enough to reflect that same light, they handed me the same curse: same mask, same story, different face. But I wasn't made to keep quiet. Because when the scapegoat learns psychology, the whole system trembles. Once you see the cycle, you can't unsee it. And once you stop carrying their lies, they collapse under their own weight.

Addiction wasn't her downfall silence was. It was how she quieted the screaming in a world that wouldn't stop taking. They stripped her piece by piece until only a shadow answered to her name.

Before she left, she gave me truth not excuses, not fairy tales. Truth her final act of love. I carry it like fire.

The day came when I had to decide if my mother would live or die. Her body was still breathing, but her spirit had been gone for years. They called me the daughter to choose: hospice or hospital, mercy or fight. I was her blood and her boundary, and no one else could make that choice. She looked at me through tired eyes and said, "It's okay, Sissy. I'm gonna come out of this." I didn't understand then. Now I do. She didn't mean she'd walk out of that hospital. She meant she'd rise out of everything that ever caged her.

She meant freedom.
She meant peace.
She meant me.

While she lay dying in Northern California, I sat in another hospital in Southern California holding my daughter's hand as machines hummed beside her. My mother and my daughter were both dying one at the end of life, one at the beginning and I was split in two. My mother already knew. She knew I'd stay with my baby; she would have wanted it that way. That was her final act of love letting me go so I could choose life.

I felt it the moment she crossed over. Not through words or sound through something deeper. The air went still. My bones went hollow. You don't have to be there to know when your mother dies; your body knows. The soul feels the shift before the mind can speak it. That's what grief feels like when it's blood-deep.

And then, as if God himself was rewriting everything, my daughter opened her eyes. She lived. And when I looked at her her face, her hair, her smile it was like seeing my mother all over again. The resemblance was almost spiritual. It was as if God had taken the woman I lost and placed her right back into my arms.

My mother didn't die; she divided her spirit between heaven and my child. The light didn't leave it moved.

There's a point in grief where pain becomes sacred, when you stop asking why and start whispering thank you. Because you realize death doesn't take someone it transforms them. I used to think my mother left me scars. Now I see she left me maps. Every wound she survived was direction. Every fall was instruction. Every silence she broke inside me became my voice.

The torch of her light was never meant to burn forever in her own hands. It was meant to be passed. She didn't leave me a burden; she left me power disguised as pain an inheritance not of weakness, but of flight.

When I say I inherited her, I don't mean her trauma. I mean her transformation her wings.

What she couldn't finish, I became.
What she lost, I reclaimed.
What they tried to bury, I resurrected.

She didn't die when her body gave out; she died when the world broke her. But her light survived long enough to find me.

And now, when I write, when I breathe, when I look at my daughter, I feel her moving through me steady, eternal, free. The one who walked through fire so I could walk through truth.

Rest in peace, Mama.
Your body's gone, but your light is eternal.
You didn't leave me ashes you left me wings.
And I finally know how to use them.

Epilogue
-For the Next Generation

There's a point after the storm when silence finally feels like peace instead of punishment.
That's where I am now.

For so long, I carried what didn't belong to me
generations of pain, secrets, lies, and shame that were never mine to hold.
I carried them because I thought I was supposed to.
Because when you grow up in survival,
you mistake endurance for love.

> **But survival isn't living.**
> **And silence isn't peace.**

My children will never have to carry what broke me.
That's the promise I made the night my mother's spirit left this world
and my daughter opened her eyes.

That was the moment I understood:
legacy isn't what you inherit
it's what you choose to pass on.

> **I will not pass down silence.**
> **I will not pass down fear.**
> **I will not pass down the belief that love must hurt to be real.**

My mother handed me her light,
and I am handing it to them
cleaned, healed,
free of the poison that dimmed her.
Pg.111

The truth is, every generation is offered a choice
repeat it or redeem it.
I chose redemption.

And that doesn't mean perfection
it means I faced the truth
and refused to let it rot in my children's bloodline.

One day they'll read these pages and understand
that I didn't write this book to expose anyone
I wrote it to set us free.

Because healing is rebellion
in a family that survives on denial.
Because truth is love
in its rawest form.
And because silence, no matter how polished,
was never protection
it was suffocation.

If my mother was the map,
then my children are the destination.
They are the life she dreamed of but never got to live.
Every time they laugh, a piece of her lives again.
Every time I love them differently, I rewrite our history.

And if one day they ever feel broken,
I want them to know this:

You come from women who were never meant to survive,
but somehow did.
You come from blood that learned to fly without wings.
You come from light
that no amount of darkness could kill.

This book isn't an ending
it's an inheritance.

NOT OF PAIN, BUT OF POWER.
Not of silence, but of voice.
And not of ashes, but of wings.

So when they ask what legacy means,
I'll tell them

It means turning what hurt you
into something that heals the world.

The Light She Left Behind

I know she was sick.
But sickness was only the shell of what was really happening.
Her body was failing, yes
but her spirit had been dying in pieces long before.

She is living proof that sometimes the soul goes first,
long before the flesh gives in.

When you look at her, don't just see the pain.
See the surrender.
Because she didn't just fade
she gave.

She gave everything she had left to give.
She didn't hoard her light;
she handed it to me in silence,
one flicker at a time,
until it lived inside my chest.

When I look at her now, I finally understand
she wasn't just dying.
She was transferring.
She was setting me free.
She was becoming the very light she gave away.

Psychologically, what she did wasn't conscious it was instinctual.
The light wasn't a thing she passed down;
it was energy, identity, resilience.
When trauma burns through generations,
some souls absorb the heat and still find a way to glow.
That's what she did.
She didn't know she was teaching me how to survive
her nervous system did.
Her spirit did.
Even as she broke, she was transmitting the blueprint of endurance,
cell by cell, breath by breath,
teaching me that survival can be inherited the same way suffering is.

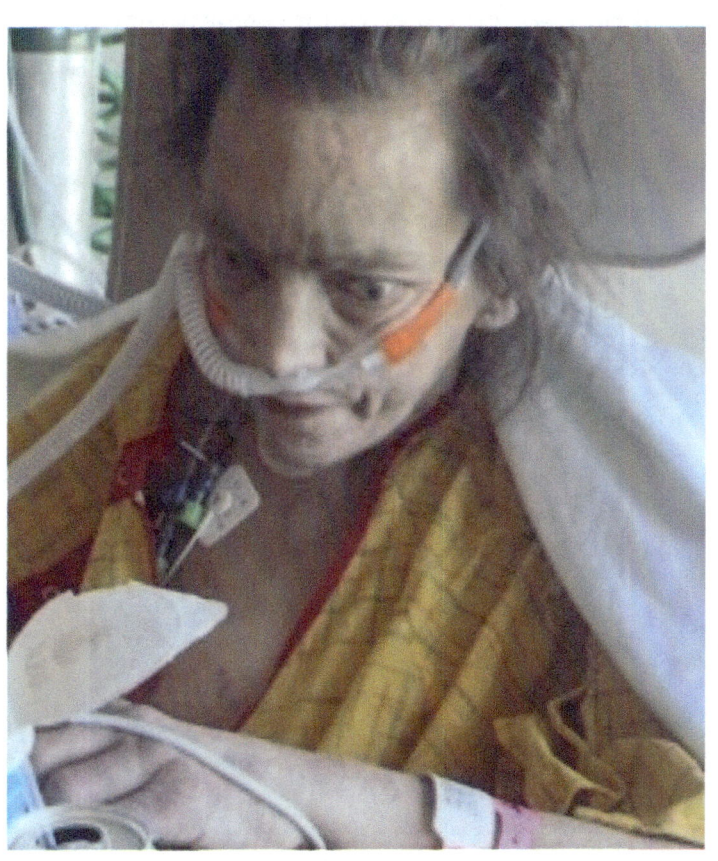

She wasn't perfect,
but the light she left wasn't either
it was wild, scarred, and trembling.
It burned unevenly, but it never went out.

It lived in me as a pulse,
a calling to finish what she started
to turn survival into living,
to turn her surrender into freedom.

And all I can say is
you really did give everything, didn't you, Mama?

Even in death,
you were still teaching me how to live.

I said my mother was punished for her light ,
but what I meant
was that she kept trying to love
what hurt her.

She thought love could fix what broke her,
that if she gave enough,
the world would finally soften.
But it didn't.

She loved through control,
through cruelty,
through silence
and it never saved them.
It only showed how deeply she still believed

in the good that never came.
In the end, it's what killed her.
And for me all I ever wanted was a family, and somehow, I
was always treated like that was too much to ask.

Author
Carissa Horton.

Made in the USA
Coppell, TX
08 February 2026

70615576R00075